Preface

Neural Connection® delivers breakthrough tools for intelligent analysis. Using Neural Connection, you can build better models to complement your traditional statistical analysis. Neural Connection includes four neural network tools and 13 other data modeling and output tools, providing flexibility for prediction, classification, time series analysis, and data segmentation.

Serial Numbers

Your serial number is your identification number with SPSS Inc. You will need this serial number when you call SPSS Inc. for information regarding support, payment, a defective diskette, or an upgraded system.

The serial number can be found on the Neural Connection diskette. Before using the system, please copy this number to the registration card.

Registration Card

Don't put it off: fill out and send us your registration card. Until we receive your registration card, you have an unregistered system. Even if you have previously sent a card to us, please fill out and return the card enclosed in your Neural Connection package. Registering your system entitles you to:

• Technical support services

• New product announcements and upgrade announcements

Customer Service

If you have any questions concerning your shipment or account, contact your local office, listed on p. vi. Please have your serial number ready for identification when calling.

Technical Support

The services of SPSS Technical Support are available to registered owners of Neural Connection. Customers may contact Technical Support for assistance in using the product or for installation help for one of the supported hardware environments.

To reach Technical Support, see the SPSS home page on the World Wide Web at *http://www.spss.com*, or call your local office, listed on p. vi. Be prepared to identify yourself, your organization, and the serial number of your system.

Tell Us Your Thoughts

Your comments are important. So send us a letter and let us know about your experiences with SPSS products. We especially like to hear about new and interesting applications using Neural Connection. Write to SPSS Inc. Marketing Department, Attn.: Director of Products Planning, 444 North Michigan Avenue, Chicago, IL 60611.

About This Manual

The *Neural Connection User's Guide* is designed to give an introduction to the Neural Connection software and a detailed description of the tools and techniques used in it. In particular, it:

- Introduces you to the features of Neural Connection

- Guides you through the installation procedure

- Explains how to start, exit, and use the basic features of the software

- Gives you a step-by-step tutorial, explaining how a problem can be solved using the NetAgent guide and the workspace

- Gives details of the functions and parameters of the tools

- Provides appendixes covering the initialization and NetAgent languages, importing and exporting SPSS files, tool algorithms, the history of neural computing, and a glossary of commonly used terms

Neural Connection® 2.0
User's Guide

SPSS Inc./Recognition Systems Inc.

For more information about SPSS® software products, please write or call

Marketing Department
SPSS Inc.
444 North Michigan Avenue
Chicago, IL 60611

Tel: (312) 329-2400
Fax: (312) 329-3668

Neural Connection® 2.0 User's Guide
Copyright © 1997 by SPSS Inc. and Recognition Systems Inc.
All rights reserved.
Printed in the United States of America.

1 2 3 4 5 6 7 8 9 0   02 01 00 99 98 97

ISBN 1-56827-150-6

Library of Congress Catalog Card Number: 96-070851

Keyboard Conventions

This *Guide* uses the following conventions for key combinations that can be used to activate commands instead of using your mouse:

- Some keys may not be labeled exactly as they are in this manual. For example, the return key is shown as **ENTER** and the Alt key as **ALT**.

- When keys are used in sequence, for example **ALT**, **F**, **O**, you should press and release each of the keys in order.

Contacting SPSS Inc.

If you would like to be on our mailing list, contact one of our offices below. We will send you a copy of our newsletter and let you know about SPSS Inc. activities in your area.

SPSS Inc.
Chicago, Illinois, U.S.A.
Tel: 1.312.329.2400
Fax: 1.312.329.3668
Customer Service:
1.800.521.1337
Sales:
1.800.543.2185
sales@spss.com
Training:
1-800-543-6607
Technical Support:
1.312.329.3410
support@spss.com

SPSS Federal Systems
Arlington, Virginia, U.S.A.
Tel: 1.703.527.6777
Fax: 1.703.527.6866

SPSS Argentina srl
Buenos Aires, Argentina
Tel: +541.816.4086
Fax: +541.814.5030

SPSS Asia Pacific Pte. Ltd.
Singapore, Singapore
Tel: +65.3922.738
Fax: +65.3922.739

SPSS Australasia Pty. Ltd.
Sydney, Australia
Tel: +61.2.9954.5660
Fax: +61.2.9954.5616

SPSS Belgium
Heverlee, Belgium
Tel: +32.162.389.82
Fax: +32.1620.0888

SPSS Benelux BV
Gorinchem, The Netherlands
Tel: +31.183.636711
Fax: +31.183.635839

SPSS Central and Eastern Europe
Woking, Surrey, U.K.
Tel: +44.(0)1483.719200
Fax: +44.(0)1483.719290

SPSS East Mediterranea and Africa
Herzelia, Israel
Tel: +972.9.526700
Fax: +972.9.526715

SPSS France SARL
Boulogne, France
Tel: +33.1.4699.9670
Fax: +33.1.4684.0180

SPSS Germany
Munich, Germany
Tel: +49.89.4890740
Fax: +49.89.4483115

SPSS Hellas SA
Athens, Greece
Tel: +30.1.7251925
Fax: +30.1.7249124

SPSS Hispanoportuguesa S.L.
Madrid, Spain
Tel: +34.1.443.3700
Fax: +34.1.448.6692

SPSS Ireland
Dublin, Ireland
Tel: +353.1.66.13788
Fax: +353.1.661.5200

SPSS Israel Ltd.
Herzlia, Israel
Tel: +972.9.526700
Fax: +972.9.526715

SPSS Italia srl
Bologna, Italy
Tel: +39.51.252573
Fax: +39.51.253285

SPSS Japan Inc.
Tokyo, Japan
Tel: +81.3.5474.0341
Fax: +81.3.5474.2678

SPSS Korea
Seoul, Korea
Tel: +82.2.552.9415
Fax: +82.2.539.0136

SPSS Latin America
Chicago, Illinois, U.S.A.
Tel: 1.312.494.3226
Fax: 1.312. 494.3227

SPSS Malaysia Sdn Bhd
Selangor, Malaysia
Tel: +603.704.5877
Fax: +603.704.5790

SPSS Mexico SA de CV
Mexico DF, Mexico
Tel: +52.5.575.3091
Fax: +52.5.575.3094

SPSS Middle East and South Asia
Dubai, UAE
Tel: +971.4.525536
Fax: +971.4.524669

SPSS Scandinavia AB
Stockholm, Sweden
Tel: +46.8.102610
Fax: +46.8.102550

SPSS Schweiz AG
Zurich, Switzerland
Tel: +41.1.201.0930
Fax: +41.1.201.0921

SPSS Singapore Pte. Ltd.
Singapore, Singapore
Tel: +65.2991238
Fax: +65.2990849

SPSS UK Ltd.
Woking, Surrey, U.K.
Tel: +44.1483.719200
Fax: +44.1483.719290

Contents

Neural Connection

Chapter 1

Overview

Neural Connection is a software system that allows you to build complex applications for solving your business problems using neural computing and other techniques.

This chapter provides the following information:

- Explains how to get started with Neural Connection

- Introduces neural computing

- Explains the structure of Neural Connection

Getting Started

The easiest way to get started with Neural Connection is by working through the tutorials provided in Chapter 4. These introduce you to the process of building applications using Neural Connection.

If you haven't installed Neural Connection yet, refer to Chapter 2, where the setup program is described.

There are two ways to build applications in Neural Connection. The first, and simplest, is to use NetAgent to load your data and build your application. NetAgent is a guide that asks you questions about your problem and uses your answers to build a solution for you. When you start Neural Connection, you can load NetAgent and use it to build an application.

To start a NetAgent demonstration:

1. On the toolbar, choose **New**.

   or

   From the File menu, choose **New**.

2. On the toolbar, click **NetAgent**.

   or

   From the NetAgent menu, choose **Run**.

3. From the samples subdirectory, select **net.agt** and click **OK**.

4. Follow the NetAgent instructions on the screen.

The second approach is to build an application manually. To do this, you must switch off NetAgent.

To stop NetAgent from running:

* In the NetAgent box, click **Stop**.

What Are Neural Networks?

At their most fundamental level, neural networks are simply a new way of analyzing your data. What makes them so useful is their ability to *learn* complex patterns and trends in your data, an ability that is unique to neural networks.

Conventional computing techniques are very good at arithmetic. They can add columns of numbers, check spellings against a dictionary, and so on. But when they are asked to do tasks such as recognizing a face, assessing a credit risk, or forecasting demand, they perform very badly.

Most of these tasks are easy for humans; indeed, some we do without conscious effort. We can recognize the face of a friend in a crowd, even when we haven't seen that friend for many years; stock market traders may make mistakes, but they are right often enough to make a profit.

Unfortunately, many of the problems faced by businesses have more in common with subjective tasks, those at which computers traditionally perform badly, than with arithmetic tasks.

In order to emulate the human ability to solve this category of problem, neural computing has abandoned conventional computing techniques and has instead concentrated on the way that biological systems, such as human brains, work.

The human brain is made up of many neurons, the brain cells, each of which is connected to many others in a network that adapts and changes as the brain learns. In neural computing, processing elements replace the neurons and these processing elements are linked together to form neural networks.

Each processing element performs a simple task. It is the connections between the processing elements that give neural networks the ability to learn patterns and inter-relationships in data.

By producing systems that learn the relationships between data and results, neural networks avoid many of the problems of conventional computing. Given new, unseen data, a neural network can make a decision or prediction based upon its experience—just as a human can.

Until recently, the benefits of neural networks were available only to people who could afford to spend time and effort becoming experts in neural computing. Neural Connection has been designed so that you can harness this technology immediately, without becoming a neural computing expert yourself.

Neural Connection Structure

Neural Connection is made up of three separate modular groups and a textual initialization language.

The modules are.

*   A graphical user interface

*   An executive

*   A set of neural network and data analysis tools

The modular design of Neural Connection gives greater flexibility than standard analysis tools and allows you to adapt your application as required, in order to gain the best results from your data.

Graphical User Interface

The graphical user interface provides the Neural Connection *workspace*, the program window where you build problem-solving applications.

The workspace allows you to build, train, and run analysis applications. An *application* is a method for modeling your problem, which may include inputting the data, processing them in some way, and producing the output in a useful format. Tools are selected as icons from a palette, and moved onto the workspace, where they can be connected to other tools. These connections determine an application's *topology*, and the path along which data flows.

The workspace has tools for inputting data, statistical analysis, problem modeling, and producing results. Each type of tool performs a specific type of task, and by combining tools in different ways, applications can be built that perform much more sophisticated analysis than any one technique could by itself.

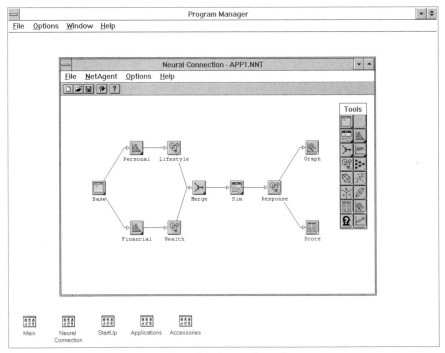

Graphical user interface

A tool that you have placed on the workspace has a series of parameters that can be set independently of other tools, even those of the same type. Initially, these parameters are set to default values that have been carefully chosen to be the optimum values for as many problems as possible. To customize these parameters, you can open each tool.

Each tool has a series of simple commands, such as **Run**, **Train**, and **Dialog**, that enables it to be used in a straightforward manner.

The Executive

The executive is the core component of Neural Connection. It creates instances of the analysis tools, displays them on the graphical user interface, and manages the data flow among them. It also loads, trains, and runs applications developed in the script language.

Tool Modules

The tool modules used by Neural Connection consist of neural network and data analysis routines that have been extensively developed. They include tools for data input and output, data manipulation, statistical analysis, classification, and modeling and forecasting. In addition to providing the standard user-defined parameters, the neural network tools contain many advanced features, such as automatic configuration and training.

The common characteristics of the analysis tools are:

*   Tools store all their data variables in a data body in your computer's memory. This allows different instances of a tool to be created by allocating new data bodies. The software associated with each tool is reentrant, allowing it to be used by all instances of the tool.

*   Tools pass data from one to another via a single logical connection. This connection passes both vector data and control information, such as the names of fields in the vector and their data types. Vector data can contain both input information and target information.

*   Tools make no assumptions about which tools are connected in front of or after them in the topology. If a tool uses the same data set many times (for example, in Multi-Layer Perceptron training), then it automatically holds the data required in memory until it is no longer needed.

Script Language

Neural Connection comes with a script language that allows you to develop any application using a text editor. It allows you to specify multiple instances of tools, set parameters to initial values, define the connections between tools, and control the training and running of the system.

Installing Neural Connection

Chapter 2

Neural Connection is provided with a setup program that automatically installs Neural Connection and its associated files onto the hard disk of your computer. Before you use Neural Connection, you must run the setup program.

This chapter explains how to set up Neural Connection on your personal computer.

Hardware and Software Requirements

Neural Connection requires the following:

- An IBM compatible PC with a 386, 486, or Pentium processor

- Microsoft DOS 5.0 or later

- Microsoft Windows 3.1 or later

- 4MB memory (8MB recommended)

- A hard disk with 4MB of free disk space

- A VGA or SVGA monitor, with appropriate graphics card

- A mouse or other pointing device

Before You Set Up Neural Connection

Before installation starts, you should check the *readme* file on the installation disk for up-to-date information about installing and using Neural Connection.

Your Neural Connection Package

Neural Connection is supplied on 3.5" disks for PC compatible computers. These supplied disks are your master copy of Neural Connection and should be stored in a safe place when not in use.

Using the Neural Connection Setup Program

To install Neural Connection:

1. If Windows is not running, type **win** at the DOS prompt and then press **ENTER.**

    or

    If Windows is running, close any open programs.

2. Insert the Neural Connection disk in the floppy disk drive (drive A).

3. From the Program Manager File menu, choose **Run (Alt, F, R)**.

4. In the text edit field, type **a:setup** and click **OK**.

5. Follow the instructions displayed on the screen.

The Neural Connection setup program checks your computer for Windows 3.1 or later and alerts you if it thinks that you are not running the program.

The setup program creates a new directory called *c:\nconnect* and places the Neural Connection software in it. If your hard drive is not the C: drive or you want to put Neural Connection in a different directory, type the full path of the directory in which you want to install Neural Connection when you are prompted during the installation process.

Section I: The Workspace

The first section of this manual gives information on how to use the workspace in the Neural Connection environment and how to use the commands and instructions related to it.

Details of the tools and their functions can be found in Section II: The Tools.

Using Neural Connection

Chapter 3

Neural Connection is a sophisticated data analysis package that uses neural networks to produce the best answers for your problems. It is designed around a development environment, the workspace, where you can create sophisticated and powerful solutions in a very simple way.

If you do not want or need to develop a complex solution, there is an intelligent guide, *NetAgent*, that helps you produce answers to your problems in a number of straightforward steps.

This chapter provides the following information:

- Explains how to start and quit Neural Connection

- Describes how to start Neural Connection from SPSS for Windows

- Explains how to create, open, and save applications in Neural Connection

- Shows you how to use the workspace

- Describes the functions available on the menu bar and toolbar

- Gives an overview of the tools

- Describes how to use NetAgent

Starting Neural Connection

The Neural Connection setup program automatically creates a Neural Connection program group, which contains the Neural Connection icon.

To start Neural Connection from Program Manager, do one of the following:

• Point at the Neural Connection icon using your mouse, and double-click your mouse button.

or

• Highlight the Neural Connection icon by using the arrow keys on your keyboard, and press **Enter.**

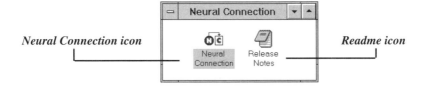

Neural Connection icon   *Readme icon*

> ***Note:*** *If the Neural Connection program group is not the active program group, hold down **Ctrl** and press **Tab** until its title bar is highlighted.*

Starting Neural Connection from SPSS for Windows

If SPSS for Windows is on your computer when Neural Connection is installed, you can start the program directly from SPSS for Windows.

Note: *The **Neural Networks** option is available only if you have opened some data in SPSS for Windows.*

To start Neural Connection from SPSS for Windows:

• From the SPSS for Windows Utilities menu, choose **Neural Networks**.

This starts Neural Connection and loads data that are open in SPSS for Windows into a Data Input tool.

Quitting Neural Connection

When you quit Neural Connection, if you have built or made changes to an application you are asked if you want to save the changes. If the application has not been named you are asked to name it.

To quit Neural Connection from the workspace:

1. From the File menu, choose **Exit** (**Alt, F, X**).

2. If an application has unsaved changes, Neural Connection asks if you want to save the application. Either click **Yes** to save your work or press **Enter** to quit without saving.

3. If the application hasn't been named, Neural Connection asks you to provide a name for the application. Type a name; your application is automatically stored with an *.nni* filename extension. (See the section on Application Names, below.)

To Quit Neural Connection from NetAgent

To quit Neural Connection while NetAgent is running, you must first stop NetAgent. To do this, follow the steps at the end of this chapter, in the section on NetAgent.

Creating Applications

Before you can work with an application, you have to create it or, if it already exists, open it.

Creating a New Application

When you start Neural Connection, a new application, temporarily named **[untitled]**, opens in the workspacc.

You can begin a new application at any time when working with Neural Connection. However, Neural Connection can operate only one application at a time and any application you are already working on will be lost unless you save it.

To create a new application:

- From the File menu, choose **New** (**Alt, F, N**).

If you are currently working on an application, Neural Connection asks if you want to save any changes to it before the new application is created.

Opening and Saving Applications

The following file is required when opening an application:

- The saved application <*filename*>.*nni*

The application is automatically given an *.nni* filename extension when you save it. The extension *.nni* simply indicates a saved application.

Note: Neural Connection cannot open applications that have been stored in an older version of Neural Connection.

Opening Existing Applications

To work on an existing application that is stored on disk, you open the application using the **Open** command on the File menu.

To open an existing application:

1. From the File menu, choose **Open** (**Alt, F, O**).

2. In the File Name box, type or select the name of the application you want to open. If you do not see the name of the application you want, select a new drive or directory.

3. Click **OK**.

Saving Open Applications

A good rule of thumb is to save every 10 to 15 minutes or after you have completed any work that you don't want to repeat. When you save an application, the application stays open on your screen, so you can keep working. When you exit Neural Connection, a message asks if you want to save changes.

To save an existing application:

- From the File menu, choose **Save** (**Alt, F, S**).

To save a new, unnamed application:

1. From the File menu, choose **Save** (**Alt, F, S**).

2. In the File Name box, type a name. (See the section on Application Names, below.)

3. If you want to save the application to a different drive or directory, do one of the following:

    •   Select a drive and a directory.

    or

    •   Type the complete path in the File Name box. For example, **c:\neural\work**.

4. Click **OK**.

If you type a filename that already exists within the directory you've designated, Neural Connection displays a message asking whether you want to replace the existing file with the active application.

Application Names

Neural Connection applications can have any acceptable filename. You can use any characters except spaces and the following characters:

    *   ?   ,   ;   [   ]   +   \   /   : | <   >

Neural Connection applications are automatically given an *.nni* extension when they are saved.

The Workspace

Using Neural Connection is an excellent way to build your data analysis applications. This section introduces you to the *workspace*, the area where problem-solving applications are built, and describes the many features and tools that enable you to get valuable results from your data.

What Is the Workspace?

The workspace is the blank canvas on which you build problem-solving applications in Neural Connection. It has its own set of commands that are called from the *menu bar*. The *toolbar* gives you shortcuts to some of the more commonly used menu bar commands. The *palette* allows you to choose tools to use on the workspace.

In Neural Connection, problems are solved using applications that are made by connecting *tools* together on the workspace.

Tools, Topologies, and Applications

Tools

Tools are the components from which you build applications. Each tool performs an action on data that are passed through it. Some tools carry out straightforward actions, while others perform intricate analyses. Tools can be connected together, allowing complex problem-solving tasks to be performed.

Topologies

The connections between tools define the paths through which data pass and the direction in which they pass. A series of connected tools is known as a *topology*.

A topology must have a pathway from an *input* tool to an *output* tool. In other words, there must be a way of getting data into the topology and a way of getting results out of the topology. Thus, the minimum valid topology is an input tool connected directly to an output tool.

The following restrictions apply to valid topologies:

- A topology must start with an input tool.

- A topology must end with an output tool.

- A topology can have only one input tool.

- Topologies cannot contain feedback loops.

A topology can have any combination of other tools between the input and output tools.

Applications

A valid topology that is being used to solve a problem is known as an *application*. It is a device that helps you get meaningful information from your data.

Applications can be very simple or exceedingly complex. Their nature depends on your data and the use to which you want to put them.

Neural Connection applications are *data driven*. A tool does not send data to a *successor* tool in your application until the successor tool requests the data. This means that data do not flow along the connections you have made until you tell the application to run.

Choosing the tools to use in an application depends on the attributes of your data and the type of problem you are trying to solve.

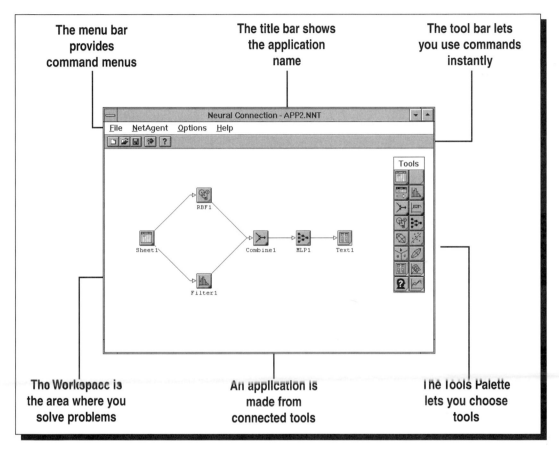

The menu bar provides command menus

The title bar shows the application name

The tool bar lets you use commands instantly

Tho Workopacc is the area where you solve problems

An application is made from connected tools

The Tools Palette lets you choose tools

The Workspace Screen

Menu Bar and Toolbar Commands

Choosing a *command* tells Neural Connection what to do next. Commands that carry out similar actions, or that are associated with particular tasks, arc grouped together in *menus,* to make finding the right command easier. For example, the File menu contains commands to open and save your networks. Four menus are listed on the menu bar at the top of the workspace window, and others are available on the Neural Connection tools.

The most commonly used menu bar commands are represented by icons on the toolbar. This enables you to activate frequently used commands simply by clicking them.

Menu Bar Commands

The commands on each menu on the menu bar can be displayed by using your mouse.

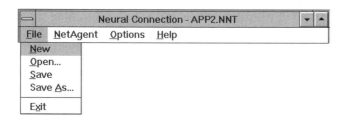

When a menu title is selected, the menu appears below the title.

To display a menu using a mouse:

• Click the menu title.

Commands on the menu bar can also be displayed using your keyboard.

To display a menu using the keyboard:

• Press **Alt** (adjacent to the space bar) followed by the underlined letter in the menu name.

Some commands may not be available all the time during your workspace session, and these will be grayed out.

To choose a command from a menu, do one of the following:

1. Point to a menu name and click the left mouse button.

2. Point to a command name and click the left mouse button.

or

1. Press **Alt** to activate the menu bar.

2. Press the underlined letter in a menu name.

3. Press the underlined letter in a command name.

If a command name is followed by an ellipsis (...), a dialog box appears, and you can set the options you require.

To Cancel a Menu

To close a menu without choosing a command, do one of the following:

- Click outside the menu.

or

- Press **ESC** to cancel the menu.

The menu bar commands are described below.

File Menu

New	Clears the workspace of any topologies that it may contain and resets Neural Connection
Open	Opens a saved topology, application or a text initialization file
Save	Saves the current application; any tools are stored with all their settings intact
Save As	Saves the current application under a different name
Exit	Quits Neural Connection

NetAgent Menu

Run	Starts a NetAgent script

Options Menu

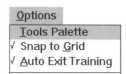

Tools Palette	Displays the tools palette
Snap to Grid	Switches the snap to grid on or off
Auto Exit Training	Automatically exits the training dialog boxes (which appear during application training) when training finishes.

Help Menu

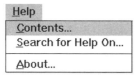

Contents	Opens the Neural Connection Help file at the contents page
Search for Help On	Allows you to use the Help index to open Help directly at a topic
About	Gives the release number of Neural Connection

Toolbar Commands

Five of the most commonly used commands are represented by icons on the toolbar. They are **New**, **Open**, **Save**, **Start from NetAgent file**, and **Help**.

 New

 Open

 Save

Start from NetAgent file

?| **Help**

To choose a Toolbar command:

• Click the command you want to use.

Using Commands

Neural Connection can carry out some commands immediately but others require more information. When more information is required, Neural Connection displays a *dialog box*.

Dialog Boxes

A dialog box is a special window containing options that tell Neural Connection how to carry out a command. The options that you select in the dialog box control how the command is carried out. There are several ways of specifying options in dialog boxes, and these are explained below.

The OK and Cancel Buttons

In many dialog boxes, the **OK** and **Cancel** command buttons appear. You select one of these buttons when you finish setting options in a dialog box.

OK   Selecting the **OK** button closes the dialog box and completes the command using the selected options. For example, selecting the **OK** button in the **Save As** dialog box starts saving the application. To select the **OK** button, you can either click the button or press **Enter.**

Cancel   Clicking the **Cancel** button discards the options you have selected, closes the dialog box, and returns you to your application.

Typing and Editing in Dialog Boxes

Some dialog boxes contain *text boxes* in which you type information or a response, such as a filename or a comment that you want to make. Others include *drop-down lists*, from which you can select from a list of options by using your mouse to click the option that you want.

To replace text in a text box:

1. Select the text you want to replace by pointing to the text box and clicking and dragging over the text.

2. Type your replacement text.

The selected text will be replaced with the new text as soon as you start typing.

To use a drop-down list:

1. Click the drop arrow at the right side of the list box. A list appears.

2. Click the option that you want.

The list is hidden and the option that you have chosen appears in the list box.

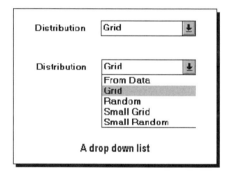

A drop down list

Tools

A tool is a method for manipulating data. All tools belong to one of four categories, or generic types. The category defines what a specific tool does, what connections it has, what data it must retain, etc.

The generic categories are:

• Input

• Filter

• Modeling and Forecasting

• Output

The icons for different tool categories have different-colored corners to enable easier identification. Input tools have red corners; Filter tools, blue; Modeling and Forecasting tools, green; and Output tools, yellow.

Tools in Neural Connection are independent of each other and make no assumptions about what other tools exist or precede or follow them. This makes the tools in Neural Connection totally interchangeable and makes Neural Connection an extremely versatile program.

Each type of tool that can be placed on the workspace has a different function and can be used as many times as you want. Each time you place a tool type on the workspace, an *instance*, a specific use, of the tool is formed that is independent of all other tools.

Once a tool has been placed on the workspace you can:

- Name the tool instance

- Connect it to other tools

- Move it to a new position

- Delete it

- Disconnect it from other tools

- Set conditions that are specific to the instance of the tool

- Examine the status of the tool instance

- Run or train an application from the tool

These functions are all available from a tool's menu, which can be accessed by clicking the tool on the workspace.

The four categories of tools are described below.

Tools for Inputting Your Data

Data Input   Imports data either from files or by cutting and pasting from other Windows applications; can be used to edit data.

See Chapter 5.1.

Tools for Outputting Your Results

Data Output   Exports data to files, displays results as text, and shows the success rate.

                           See Chapter 6.1.

Text Output   Displays results as text and shows the success rate.

                           See Chapter 6.2.

Graphics Output   Displays a graph showing how the output from an application varies when two of the inputs vary.

                           See Chapter 6.3.

What If?   Displays a plot of how the output varies when two of the inputs vary and gives a description of how the change in one input affects the output.

                           See Chapter 6.4.

Time Series Plot   Displays the results of time series prediction against time.

                           See Chapter 6.5.

Tools for Modeling and Forecasting

Multi-Layer Perceptron

A neural network modeling tool that is optimized for prediction applications.

See Chapter 7.1.

Radial Basis Function

A neural network modeling tool that is optimized for prediction and classification applications.

See Chapter 7.2.

Bayesian Network

A neural network modeling tool that is optimized for prediction and classification applications.

See Chapter 7.3.

Kohonen Network

A neural network modeling tool that is optimized for clustering applications.

See Chapter 7.4.

Closest Class Means Classifier

A statistical modeling tool that can be use for classification applications.

See Chapter 7.5.

Regression   A statistical modeling tool that can be used for prediction problems.

See Chapter 7.6.

Principal Component Analysis   A statistical modeling tool that can be used to reduce the complexity of an application.

See Chapter 7.7.

Tools for Filtering Your Data

Filter   A tool that allows you to filter your data, apply mathematical functions, and examine the statistical distribution of your data.

See Chapter 8.1.

Network Combiner A tool that allows you to join two or more other tools together.

See Chapter 8.2.

Simulator   A tool that produces the data format needed by the Graphics Output and What If? tools.

See Chapter 8.3.

Time Series Window   A tool that allows you to manipulate time series data in order to create windows before modeling takes place.

See Chapter 8.4.

Using Tools

Tools become active when they are placed on the workspace.

To place a tool on the workspace:

1. Select a tool type from the tool palette by clicking it with your mouse.

2. Move your mouse to the desired place on the workspace.

3. Click your mouse button to place the tool on the workspace.

Tools can be moved to a new position once they have been placed on the workspace.

To move a tool on the workspace:

•   Click and drag the tool to new position.

Tool Commands

The Neural Connection tools have certain commands in common and these can be accessed from a tool's menu by clicking on the tool. Each tool has its own menu, which enables you to control it independently.

Tools obey the following commands:

Connect	Connects one tool to another
Delete	Removes the tool from the workspace
Dialog	Sets up preferences in a tool
Disconnect	Removes all inputs to, and outputs from, a tool
Name	Names an instance of a tool
Run	Runs an application connected to a tool

Status	Displays the status of a tool
Train	Trains a tool to use its data
View	Opens the Data Input and the Data Output tools

To access a tool's menu:

• Click the tool.

Deleting Tools

Tools can be removed from the workspace by using the **Delete** command.

*Note: If you use the **Delete** command to remove a tool that has been placed on the workspace, all the connections to and from it are disconnected.*

To delete a tool:

• From the tool menu, choose **Delete**.

Connecting Tools

Tools are connected by using the **Connect** command. Connections are always made from the upstream tool to the downstream tool and are indicated by a line between the two tools, with an arrow to show the direction of data flow.

To connect two tools:

1. From the upstream tool's menu, choose **Connect**.

2. Click the downstream tool.

If you choose the **Connect** command by mistake, it is possible to drop the connection.

To drop the connection:

• Click the tool from which you chose the **Connect** command.

Disconnecting Tools

Tools can be disconnected from a topology by using the **Disconnect** command. When the **Disconnect** command is used, all connections to and from the tool are removed.

To disconnect tools:

• Fom the tool menu of either tool, choose **Disconnect**.

Tool Instance Names

Each instance of a tool that is placed on the workspace is given a name. Initially, this name is *Tool X*, where *Tool* is the type of tool and *X* is a number—for example, Input 1 or Text Output 4. You can customize your application by renaming the tool instances that you have placed in the workspace.

To change a tool instance name:

1. On the tool menu, choose **Name**.

2. In the instance box, type a name.

3. Click **OK**.

Tool Settings

As you build an application, you will need to change the settings of the different tool instances in order to best solve your problem. To adjust the settings, choose the **Dialog** command. Each type of tool has its own adjustable settings, and these are discussed in detail in the following chapters.

To view the current status of a tool:

• From the tool menu, choose **Status**. A list of all the tool's adjustable settings appears.

NetAgent

To help you to build your first Neural Connection applications, a guide called *NetAgent* has been provided. NetAgent has been written using the NetAgent language detailed in Appendix I.

A full description of how to use NetAgent is given in the first tutorial in Chapter 4.

To load NetAgent:

1. Start Neural Connection.

2. From the NetAgent menu, choose **Run**.

   or

   On the toolbar, click **NetAgent**.

3. From the samples subdirectory, select **net.agt**.

4. Click **OK.**

When you start NetAgent, it displays a message and two buttons, **Play** and **Stop**.

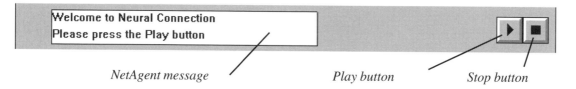

NetAgent message   *Play button*   *Stop button*

The buttons have the following functions:

Play   Moves NetAgent on to the next stage. If you have been asked for an answer to a question, the answer you have given will be accepted by NetAgent when you click this button.

Stop   Exits NetAgent and returns you to the workspace. If you have used NetAgent to build an application, you will be able to use the application on the workspace.

NetAgent asks you questions in two different ways. It asks you either to enter text in a text edit field or to choose one of several options in a drop-down list. In both cases, after responding by typing text or selecting an option from a drop-down list, you must click **Play**.

To quit Neural Connection from NetAgent:

1. In NetAgent, click **Stop**.

2. From the File menu, choose **Exit (Alt, F, X)**.

3. If an application has unsaved changes, Neural Connection asks if you want to save the application. Either click **Yes** to save your work or press **Enter** to quit without saving.

4. If the application hasn't been named, Neural Connection asks you to provide a name for the application. Your application is automatically stored with an *.nni* filename extension.

Tutorials

Chapter 4

This chapter guides you through two tutorials that show you how to solve the same problem in different ways. The first tutorial uses NetAgent, Neural Connection's intelligent guide, to solve the problem. The second shows you how to build the same solution and get the same results by building an application manually on the workspace. The second tutorial looks at the problem in more detail and introduces some of the issues that are covered in the *Neural Connection Applications Guide*. (Descriptions of other applications can also be found in the *Applications Guide*.)

This chapter provides the following information:

- Describes the problem

- Guides you through the first tutorial

- Guides you through the second tutorial

The Problem

Direct marketing is an area in which neural computing has had considerable success. In direct marketing, a product or service is sold by sending an offer directly to the customer; there is no shop, agent, or broker between the company that sells the product and the customer who purchases it. This process can give higher profits than conventional selling techniques, but since the cost of mailing an offer to a potential customer is high, it is important that each offer be targeted as accurately as possible.

Neural computing has proved to be an excellent way of targeting such offers. It is able to analyze the complex relationships between customers' attributes and customers' likely responses to an offer.

This chapter presents a problem faced by a mail order company. The company sold goods to its customers through direct marketing and was about to launch a new product. The company wanted to know which of its existing customers would respond to this new offer.

Aims

By predicting people who would respond, the company hoped to cut the cost of the mailing, without a corresponding loss of custom.

To solve this problem, you will build an application that predicts whether a customer falls into one of two categories:

- Those that will respond to the offer

- Those that will not

At the end, you will produce a measure of the success—a percentage of customers correctly classified—that is based on customer records to which your application will not have had access originally.

How Were the Data Collected?

The company had launched a similar product one year before and had recorded which customers responded to that offer and which did not. By including information that they had on their customer database, the company was able to build a data set that had the following information for each customer:

- Age

- Nearest regional office

- Number of orders made in the last quarter

- Amount of money spent on orders in the last year

- Date at which they first purchased through the company

- Response to the launch of the similar product

How Will the Problem Be Solved?

You will build an application that learns to associate the response of a customer with the customer's age, region, number of orders, total yearly expenditure, and date of joining the company. The neural network in your application will build a model of these associations that will enable it to predict the response of customers in advance. The inputs to the neural network will be the five pieces of biographical information given above, and the output will be the response of the customer.

NetAgent Tutorial

To solve the problem using NetAgent:

1. Start Neural Connection by double-clicking the Neural Connection icon.

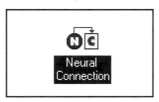

2. Start NetAgent by clicking **NetAgent** and selecting **net.agt** from the samples subdirectory.

3. Step NetAgent forward by clicking **Play** until NetAgent asks if you want to run in the **Beginner** or **Advanced** mode.

If this is the first time you have used NetAgent, you may want to use the Beginner mode. This mode provides additional information about the decisions you will have to make.

To select the Beginner mode:

1. Click the drop-down list. A list appears.

2. Click **Beginner**.

3. Click **Play**.

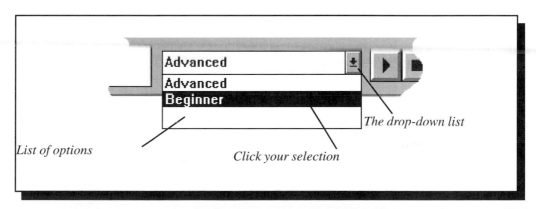

The next question asked is whether your problem is a classification problem or a prediction problem.

A *classification* problem is one where the model decides which of a number of categories it should select when it is shown an example. A *prediction* problem is one where the model chooses a numerical value when it is shown an example.

This problem is a classification problem. You are trying to decide whether an example (a potential customer) belongs to a class of responders or to a class of non-responders.

To specify a classification problem:

1. Step NetAgent forward by clicking **Play** until you are asked if your problem is a classification or prediction problem.

2. Use the drop down list to select **Classification**.

3. Click **Play**.

NetAgent next asks you to choose either a neural or a statistical solution. If you choose a neural solution, NetAgent will use a neural network to solve your problem. If you choose a statistical solution, NetAgent will use a classical statistical technique to solve your problem. The neural network that is used in this NetAgent script is the Radial Basis Function; the statistical techniques that are used are the Closest Class Mean Classifier and the Regression tool.

 Radial Basis Function neural network.
See Chapter 7.2.

 Closest Class Mean Classifier.
See Chapter 7.5.

 Regression Tool.
See Chapter 7.6.

If this is the first time that you have used NetAgent, we suggest that you choose a neural technique. You may want to run through this script again later and choose a linear technique, in order to compare results.

To choose a neural technique:

1. Use the drop-down list to select **Neural**.

2. Click **Play**.

NetAgent needs to know the name of the data file to use for training and for testing the model that it will build. Normally, you should ensure that this file has been moved or copied to the directory that contains Neural Connection. For this tutorial, the data file that you will use, called *tutor.sav*, is already in the correct directory.

To specify the filename:

1. Step NetAgent forward by clicking **Play** until you are asked for the name of the data file.

2. Click the text entry field and type the name of the data file, *tutor.sav*.

3. Click **Play**.

NetAgent asks which data set you will want to examine when you view the results from your model. You can choose from three data sets: *training*, *validation*, or *test* data.

• Training data are used to train your application.

• Validation data are used to monitor performance during training.

• Test data are used to measure the performance of a trained application.

Since you want to measure the performance of the model on the problem, you should use the test data set.

To specify the test data set:

1. Use the drop-down list to select the **Test** data.

2. Click **Play**.

Next NetAgent trains the model that you have chosen. During training, a window showing the progress made during training appears.

To train the model:

• Step NetAgent forward until training begins.

Once training has finished, NetAgent stops. This leaves you on the workspace and enables you to view the results from running your application.

To see results:

• From the Results tool menu, choose **View**.

You can now move on to the second part of the tutorial, where you will build the same application without the help of NetAgent.

Workspace Tutorial

This tutorial looks at the problem faced by the mail order company in more detail. It introduces issues that are developed in the *Applications Guide*, and shows how some of the principals of application development are applied in Neural Connection.

Developing a neural solution to a problem can be broken down into a number of steps:

Preproject: Setting project goals and establishing the desired results and system requirements

Data Collection: Ensuring that the correct data are gathered

Data Preparation: Cleaning the data and ensuring that they are in the appropriate format for Neural Connection

Design: Choosing the best neural approach

Training and Testing: Building your application

Experimentation: Tailoring the application to improve your results

Implementation: Producing your results

In this tutorial, you will look at each of these stages in turn, building the application in Neural Connection as you go.

Preproject

Before you start to develop an application in Neural Connection, it is important to assess what you hope to achieve. When the mail order company examined their problem in detail, they decided that they wanted to take a different approach from the one used in the first tutorial.

In the first tutorial, the problem was solved by putting customers into one of two categories, responders and non-responders. A better approach for the company was to re-code the problem so that responders were represented by 1.0, and non-responders by 0.0. The model built in Neural Connection would then be able to produce a *probability* of a customer responding.

This was much more useful because the customers could be scored according to this probability and ranked in the order of their likelihood of responding. A number of different strategies could then be investigated in order to produce the best cost/benefit scenario for the company.

Data Collection

The mail order company split their data into two sections:

- Data collected during the previous campaign, to be used for training and testing

- Data from the current customer database, to be scored and used in the new campaign

The data for training and testing are represented by the data file *tutor.sav*. The customer database data are represented by the data file *tutor_rn.sav*.

Data Preparation

When collecting data for training and testing, the mail order company had to ensure that the data were in the same format as the data that would be available when their new campaign was launched. To successfully run Neural Connection, it is important that the same data fields exist and that they be encoded in the same way.

Design

The first consideration in designing the application is the neural technique to be adopted. This type of problem, in which you want to link a set of inputs (customer features) to an output (customer response), should be solved using a *supervised* neural technique. There are three supervised neural techniques in Neural Connection: *Radial Basis Function*, the *Bayesian Network,* and *Multi-Layer Perceptron*.

The mail order company decided to use the Radial Basis Function.

The second consideration is the type of output desired. Because initial results would be examined using a cross tabulation matrix and a test data set, the *Text Output* was selected. Because the results from the application were to be fed back into the customer database, a *Data Output* was needed. Because the company also wanted to investigate the model that was built by using visualization, a *Graphics Output* was selected.

The final design consisted of:

 Data Input for importing data

 Filter for use during experimentation

 Simulator tool to enable the use of visualization

 Radial Basis Function, a neural network technique to build the model

 Text Output to examine results

 Data Output to output results

 Graphics Output to examine the neural model

Once the design is complete, the application can be built, and training and testing can start.

Training, Testing, and Experimentation

To start the application do one of the following:

- If Neural Connection is not running, start it by double-clicking the Neural Connection icon.

or

- If Neural Connection is already running, from the File menu, choose **New**.

You will use the Data Input tool to enter the data that will be used to solve the problem. For more information on the Data Input tool, see Chapter 5.1.

To select the Data Input tool and place it on the workspace:

1. From the Tools Palette, click the Data Input tool.
2. Move your mouse to the left side of the workspace.
3. Place the tool on the left side of the workspace by clicking your mouse button.

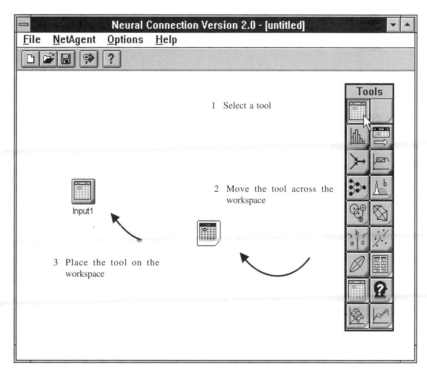

Placing a tool on the workspace

If you want to move the Data Input or any other tool on the workspace:

1. Point your mouse at the tool.

2. Hold down the left mouse button.

3. Move the tool to the correct position using your mouse.

4. Release the mouse button.

Next, you will load the training data for the problem. The data have been stored in the data file *tutor.sav* in the same directory as Neural Connection. To load the data, you must open the Data Input tool, and tell it to open *tutor.sav*.

To load the training data:

1. Click the Data Input tool once. The Data Input tool menu appears.

Data Input tool menu

2. From the Data Input tool menu, choose **View**. A blank spreadsheet appears.

Data Viewer - [Input development data]						
File Edit Data Field Window						
	Integer	I	Integer	I	Integer	I
	var0000		var0001		var0002	
14						
15						
16						
17						
18						
19						
20						
21						
22						
23						
24						
25						
26						
Ready					NUM	SCRL

Blank spreadsheet

3. From the File menu, choose **Open**. The Data Input dialog box appears. This box allows you to specify the development data file and the run data file, which are loaded separately. The development data file will be used to train and test the application. The run data file will be used when the model is implemented.

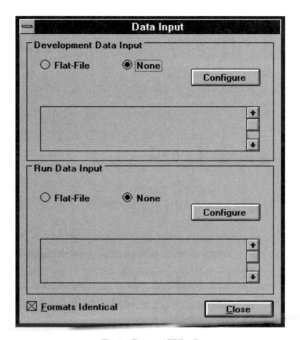

Data Input Window

4. In the Development Data Input group, click **Flat-File**.

5. Click **Configure**. A File Open window appears.

6. Do one of the following:

   • Type **tutor.sav** in the **File Name** field and click **OK**,

   or

   • Select **tutor.sav** from the list of files below the **File Name** field and click **OK**.

The data are now loaded into the Data Input tool. The Data Input assumes that the last field loaded is the field containing the output data, and that the other fields are inputs. The Data Input tool also automatically selects the data elements that are to be used to train, validate, and test the model.

Field type button

		Float	I	Symbol	I	Float	I	Float	I	Float	I	Symbol	T
		VAR_0001		VAR_0002		VAR_0003		VAR_0004		VAR_0005		VAR_0006	
1	T	56.0		Guildford		90.620003		1.0		90.695679		non-resp	
2	T	28.0		Glasgow		80.0		1.0		90.695679		respond	
3	T	38.0		London		200.0		3.0		90.6446		non-resp	
4	T	35.0		Cardiff		80.0		1.0		90.695679		respond	
5	T	38.0		Glasgow		320.0		1.0		90.6446		respond	
6	T	36.0		London		110.0		1.0		91.0989		respond	
7	T	31.0		Cambridge		170.0		2.0		90.639229		non-resp	
8	T	28.0		Guildford		290.0		3.0		90.639229		non-resp	
9	T	34.0		London		620.005005		2.0		91.442993		non-resp	
10	T	42.0		London		260.0		1.0		90.6446		respond	
11	T	49.0		Cambridge		255.255005		4.0		90.695679		non-resp	
12	T	28.0		Manchester		357.140015		2.0		91.445679		non-resp	
13	T	56.0		London		80.0		1.0		90.639229		respond	
14	T	56.0		Birmingham		80.0		1.0		90.695679		respond	
15	T	43.0		London		200.0		2.0		90.6446		non-resp	
16	T	58.0		London		230.0		2.0		90.835457		non-resp	
17	T	65.0		London		134.0		2.0		91.362343		non-resp	
18	T	38.0		Cambridge		82.699997		1.0		90.639229		respond	
19	T	39.0		Guildford		320.0		2.0		90.6446		non-resp	
20	T	50.0		Birmingham		80.0		1.0		90.639229		respond	

Tutor.sav spreadsheet

In the *tutor.sav* file, the output has been coded as a symbolic field. (As shown above, the field type button for the output field says **Symbol**, indicating a symbolic field.) It has two values, *respond* and *non-resp*. Remember that in the Preproject stage, the mail order company decided that it wanted to predict a numerical value rather than give a symbolic decision. To do this, the output field must be changed to a numeric field, with the *non-resp* symbol converted to 0.0 and *respond* converted to 1.0.

To change the field type to numeric:

1. Click the field type button. The Field Conversion dialog box opens.

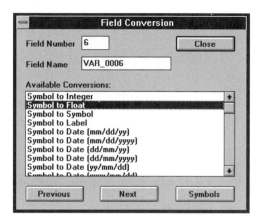

Field Conversion dialog box

2. Click **Symbols**. This opens the Symbol Editor.

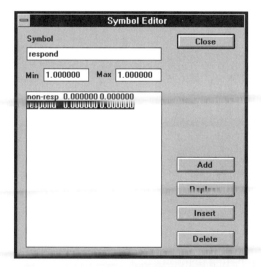

Symbol Editor

3. Highlight the **respond** symbol.

4. Change the **Min** and **Max** windows to 1.0.

5. Click **Replace**.

6. Click **Close**. The Field Conversion window reappears.

7. Under Available Conversions, click **Symbol to Float**.

8. Click **Close**. The values in the field change to 1.0 and 0.0.

You can now leave the Data Input tool. (For further information on the Data Input tool, see Chapter 5.1.)

To close the Data Input window:

• From the Data Input File menu, choose **Exit & Return**.

You can now build the rest of your application. For this problem, you are going to use a Filter, a Simulator, a Radial Basis Function neural network, a Graphics Output tool, a Data Output tool, and a Text Output tool.

To get the tools ready to use:

1. Place a Filter tool on the workspace to the right of the Data Input.

2. Place a Simulator tool on the workspace to the right of the Filter tool.

3. Place a Radial Basis Function on the workspace to the right of the Simulator tool.

4. Place a Text Output tool on the workspace to the right of the Radial Basis Function.

5. Place a Data Output tool on the workspace to the right of the Radial Basis Function.

6. Place a Graphics Output on the workspace tool below the Text Output tool.

The next step is to connect the tools together, to create the path along which data will flow when you run the application.

To connect the Data Input to the Filter tool:

1. Click the Data Input tool.

2. From the tool's menu, choose **Connect**.

3. Click the Filter tool.

A connection now points from the Data Input to the Filter.

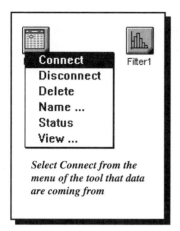
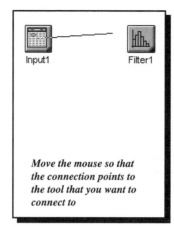
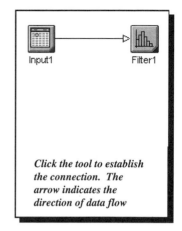

Select Connect from the menu of the tool that data are coming from

Move the mouse so that the connection points to the tool that you want to connect to

Click the tool to establish the connection. The arrow indicates the direction of data flow

Connecting tools

4. Follow the previous three steps to connect the following tools:

- The Filter to the Simulator

- The Simulator to the Radial Basis Function

- The Radial Basis Function to the Text Output

- The Radial Basis Function to the Data Output

- The Radial Basis Function to the Graphics Output

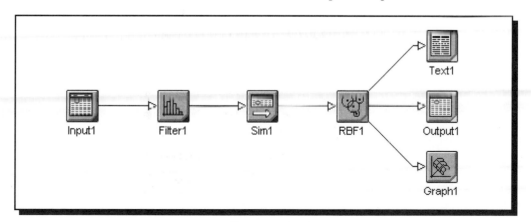

Connected tools

Note: *If you make a mistake while connecting tools, you can remove all the connections to and from a tool by selecting* Disconnect *from the tool's menu.*

The final task before running the application from the Text Output is to alter the format in which the results are produced. Running the Text Output produces a Cross Tabulation Matrix and percentage correct. For this problem, the most significant indicator of success is correctly deciding if a customer is more likely to respond to the campaign or not. The statistics in the Text Output can be altered to reflect this by using a cross tabulation matrix with two bins, one between 0.0 (more likely to respond) and 0.5 (more likely not to respond), and one between 0.5 and 1.0.

To change the statistics in the Text Output:

1. Click the Text Output.

2. From the Text Output menu, choose **Dialog**.

3. In the Data Output dialog box, select **Format**.

4. In the Output Format dialog box, type **2** into the **Bins** text edit field.

5. In the Output Format dialog box, click **OK**.

6. Click **OK**.

You can now run the application, and produce your results. Neural Connection automatically selects parameters for the neural network. While the Radial Basis Function is training, the Training Dialog box appears. When training is complete, the results appear on the screen.

To run the application:

• From the Text Output menu, choose **Run**.

When you have viewed the results, you can leave the results screen.

To leave the results screen:

• From the menu bar, click **Text Display Off!** .

```
!
! Input Data Set : Test
!
! Tue Oct 29 13:38:10 1996
!
!** Data **
!
!Record No. Input Field                                      Target Field   Output Field
!           VAR_1      VAR_2       VAR_3    VAR_4    VAR_5     RBF1           RBF1
!
1           35.0       Guildford   140.0    1.0      91.0989   0.0            0.63489
2           26.0       London      200.0    2.0      91.44568  0.0            0.26208
3           23.0       Cardiff     170.0    1.0      90.6446   1.0            0.81645
4           43.0       Cambridge    20.0    1.0      90.69568  1.0            0.70022
5           27.0       Cambridge    80.0    1.0      90.63923  1.0            0.74891
6           70.0       Cardiff     170.0    2.0      90.63923  0.0            0.40112
7           54.0       London      770.0    3.0      91.26826  0.0            0.08399
8           32.0       Plymouth    290.0    2.0      91.44568  0.0            0.32302
...
380         65.0       Guildford    80.0    1.0      90.78976  1.0            0.59945
381         50.0       Cambridge   140.0    1.0      90.63923  0.0            0.54198
382         43.0       London      140.0    1.0      91.44568  0.0            0.61266
!
!   ** Cross Tabulation Matrix For Output 1 **
!
! True           Predicted
! ----           ---------
!                0.0+ 0.5+
! 0.0+           134  66   ─────────────────────── Cross tabulation matrix
! 0.5+            48  134
!
! Total number of targets : 382
!
! Total correct : 268
!
! Percentage correct : 70.16%  ──────────── Percentage of examples correctly classified
```

Application results

The results achieved in this first pass were good, but the mail order company wanted to improve on them. One way to achieve this is by preprocessing the data. In Neural Connection, this can be accomplished by using the Filter tool to analyze and weight data fields.

When the company analyzed the third field (the amount of money spent in the last year), they discovered that it was heavily skewed to the left.

To analyze the third field:

1. Click the Filter tool.

2. From the Filter menu, choose **Dialog**.

3. Click **Var_3**.

4. Click **Analyze**.

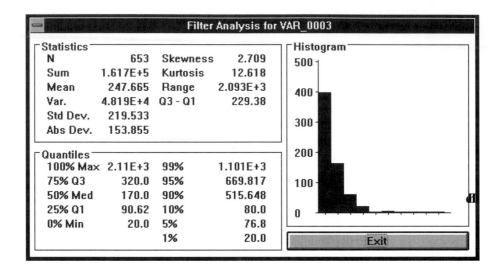

Analysis window

The values in the field can be weighted to make the distribution more normal. This will help the Radial Basis Function solve the problem. Because the field is skewed to the left, an appropriate function would be a logarithmic function.

To weight the third field:

1. In the Analysis window, click **Exit**.

2. Click the weighting function cell in the Var_3 column.

3. To access the weighting functions, click the arrow button next to the text entry field at the top left of the window.

4. Click **ln(x+a)**.

5. Reanalyze the field by clicking **Analyze**.

Once the field has been weighted, you should close the Filter tool and rerun the application to see if the results have improved.

To rerun the application that you have built:

•   From the Text Output menu, choose **Run**.

When you have viewed the results, you can leave the results screen.

To leave the results screen:

• From the menu bar, click **Text Display Off!**.

When the mail order company were satisfied with the results that they were producing, they wanted to examine the relationships between inputs and outputs detected by the neural network. To do this, they would graph two of the input variables—customer age, and number of purchases in the past year—against the output produced by the neural network.

To select the inputs to display, you use the Simulator tool.

To set up the variables to be examined in the Simulator:

1. Click the Simulator tool.

2. From the Simulator menu, choose **Dialog**.

3. In the Var_1 column, set the **Scan Order** to 1 and the **Num Values** to 21.

4. In the Var_4 column, set the **Scan Order** to 2 and the **Num Values** to 21.

5. Select **Simulator Enabled**.

6. Click **OK**.

This enables the application to produce a plot of Var_1 (customer age) and Var_4 (number of purchases in the past year) against the likelihood of responding.

To produce the graph, you run the Graphics Output tool. To do this:

• From the Graphics Output menu, choose **Run**.

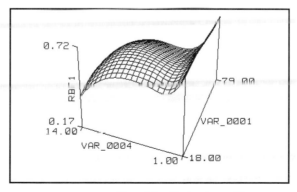

Graphics Output results

When you have viewed the graph, you can leave the results screen. To do this:

- From the menu bar, click **Graphics Display Off!**.

Next, you switch off the Simulator. To do this:

1. Click the **Simulator** tool.

2. From the Simulator menu, choose **Dialog**.

3. Deselect **Simulator Enabled**.

4. Click **OK**.

Implementation

After the mail order company examined the graphical results they had produced, the application was saved and the implementation phase started.

During implementation, no further training takes place and records from the customer database are passed through the application. Each customer record that is passed through the application generates an output and this output is used to rank the customers in order of their likelihood of response.

The customer database file can now be loaded as a run file. To load the file *tutor_rn.sav* into the Data Input as run data:

1. Click the Data Input.

2. From the Data Input menu, choose **View**.

3. From the File menu, choose **Open**. The Data Input window appears. This window allows you to specify the run file, which is loaded separately from the development file.

4. In the Run box, click **Flat File**.

5. Click **Configure**. A File Open window appears.

6. In the File Name field, type **tutor_rn.sav**.

7. Click **OK**.

Next, you close the Data Input. To do this:

- From the File menu, choose **Exit & Return**.

The application can now be run and results can be directed to an SPSS for Windows file. This is done using the Data Output tool.

The Data Output tool is more complex than the Text Output tool. It can produce Cross Tabulation Matrices and view the output from the development and run data.

To direct the results to an SPSS file:

1. Click the Data Output tool.

2. From the File menu, choose **View**. A blank spreadsheet opens.

3. From the File menu, choose **Setup**. The Data Output window appears. In this window, you specify where data from the development and run files should be written.

4. In the Run Data Output group, click **Flat-File**.

5. Click **Configure**. A Save As window opens.

6. Specify the name and type of file to be written.

7. Click **OK**.

8. In the Data Output window, click **Close**.

Before you can run the data to a file, you must view it in the Data Output tool.

• From the **View** menu, choose **Run**.

To run the application:

• From the Data Viewer File menu, choose **Output Run Data**.

The results are produced as *results.sav*, as well as appearing on the screen.

The mail order company then ranked their customer database according to the outputs produced by the neural network. When they launched a new direct marketing campaign, they found that they were able to reduce the size of their mailing by 20%, while retaining 96% of their expected response.

Conclusion

This concludes the second Neural Connection tutorial. For further information on building and deploying applications, please see the *Applications Guide*.

Section II: The Tools

The second section of this *Guide* gives details of the tools that are available in Neural Connection and how they can be used.

The chapters have been divided into four groups, each relating to one of the four tool categories: Input, Output, Modeling and Forecasting, and Filter.

Chapter Format

Each chapter follows this format:

- **Overview**

  A brief description of the tool, a list of topics covered in the chapter, and a guide to when the tool may be useful

- **How to use the tool**

  A guide to the basic functionality of the tool; how to use the tool

- **Advanced features**

  How to improve your use of the tool

- **Saved Settings**

  A sample ASCII text file containing the initialization commands for the tool

Input Tools

Chapter 5

Overview

An input tool is the mechanism for getting your data into Neural Connection. Neural Connection has one input tool, the Data Input tool. Chapter 5.1, Data Input Tool, explains how to use the Input tool.

This chapter provides the following information:

- Describes the input data formats that Neural Connection can recognize

- Explains how your data must be organized before they are entered into Neural Connection

Note: In the following descriptions, a field *refers to a column of data that describes one feature of the data set, and a* record *refers to one unit, or row, of the data set, which may contain several fields.*

Data Set Size

Neural Connection has upper limits on the amount of data that can be used. The limits differ for training and running models.

For training, the limits are:

- A maximum of 750 fields

- A maximum of 15,000 records

For running the model, the limits are:

• A maximum of 750 fields

• A maximum of 32,000 records

Data Format

Before you can use the Input tool, you must make sure that your data are presented in a way that Neural Connection can accept. Your data may have been collected in a number of different ways and may have been entered into a spreadsheet program such as Microsoft Excel or Lotus 1-2-3, or into a database or other program. Whatever their collection method, however, it is important that you extract data from your source in a format that Neural Connection can read.

Neural Connection accepts input data files in the following formats:

.Nna Files   *Field count data* (*.nna* filename extension). Field count data are presented in ASCII flat file format, with each input or output value represented by a data field. Fields may be separated by spaces, commas, or returns. New line instructions are ignored, allowing records to extend over more than one line. Field count data cannot contain missing data that are specified by null entries. User defined missing values can be set up normally using the Data Input tool.

.Csv and .Txt Files   *Record delimited data* (*.csv* or *.txt* filename extension). Record delimited data fields are separated by delimiting characters, commas, or spaces. Records are delimited by new line characters. The number of fields in a record is computed from the first logical line of data.

SPSS Files   *SPSS file format data* (*.sav* filename extension). SPSS for Windows 6.0 and 7.0 files can be read. For further information on how SPSS data types are handled, please see Appendix II, SPSS File Conversion.

Systat Files   *Systat file format data* (*.sys* filename extension). Systat version 5.05 files can be read.

Excel Files   *Excel worksheet data* (*.xls* filename extension). Microsoft Excel 5.0 files can be read.

The Excel worksheet must meet the following conditions:

- It must be the first worksheet in Excel.
- It must not contain embedded objects or graphics.
- It must not be password protected.

Data Types

Neural Connection can read five types of data:

- Integer
- Floating point
- Symbolic
- Year-date
- Day-date

For decision problems, you must use a symbolic data type for the output, with a different symbol for each decision class. For prediction problems, you must use an integer or floating point data type for each output.

Input data fields may contain data of any of these five data types. Neural Connection automatically determines the data type for each input value by parsing the first line in the data file.

Integer

Neural Connection can recognize any integer in the range -2 147 483 647 to 2 147 483 647. However, it is best not to use numbers with more than seven digits. This is because eight digit numbers start to lose resolution within Neural Connection. For example, the numbers 21 474 899, 21 474 900, and 21 474 901 are all taken to have the same value: 21 474 900.

Floating Point

Neural Connection recognizes floating point numbers, including a decimal point and a maximum of eight digits, optionally preceded by plus or minus signs. As with integer data, care should be taken when using long numbers to avoid loss of resolution.

Symbolic

Neural Connection recognizes labels containing any alphanumeric characters as *symbolic* fields. Symbolic fields are interpreted as literal strings of characters. Thus, Neural Connection classifies *GOOD* as different from *good*.

Symbolic data have a maximum length of 14 characters. When loading data in formats that allow longer symbolic strings, Neural Connection truncates the entries.

Scientific Notation

Neural Connection can recognize data that have been written in scientific notation, as long as they follow a specific format. A number written in scientific notation has two parts, the mantissa and the exponent:

```
2.135678      x 10³⁴
Mantissa      x 10^Exponent
```

Neural Connection reads scientific notation if it adheres to the following format:

```
± Mantissa e ±Exponent
```

The following examples are valid numbers:

```
2e3           2000
3.4E-2        0.034
-9e-1         -0.9
9e            9.0      (the exponent of zero is assumed)
2.16E2.5      216.0    (the fractional part of the exponent is
                        ignored)
```

Development Data

The set of data used to build and optimize your application is known as *training data*. For decision problems, it should ideally contain approximately the same number of examples of each decision. For prediction problems, the data should be well distributed over the output range.

You *could* use the whole file of data to train an application, but how would you know what performance to expect from the trained application? One solution is to set aside part of your data file as a *test* set to measure the performance of the trained application.

During training, neural techniques need to have some way of evaluating their own performance. Since they are learning to associate the inputs from the training file with the outputs, evaluating the performance of the application on the training data may not produce the best results from the system. This is because, if a network is allowed to train for too long, it *overtrains*; that is, it loses its ability to generalize. To allow the neural computing technique to monitor its performance in a more sensible fashion, another part of the data is set aside as a *validation* set.

This gives us three subsets of the data:

- Training data: used to train your application

- Validation data: used to monitor neural network performance during training

- Test data: used to measure the performance of a trained application

Note: When an application is used to predict answers for a test data set in which the actual results are not known, the test set is sometimes known as the run *data set. Run data do not have any target outputs.*

In the Data Input tool, the split between training, test, and validation data can be achieved in the viewer. You can also load run data into the Data Input tool.

Note: Unless you are modeling a time series problem, it is important that you choose the test data randomly from the overall data file. If you choose the test file based on any other criterion, you will obtain biased estimates of the performance.

How much of the file should you use for training and how much should you reserve for testing? This depends on how much data you have available. There is little point in designing an application with 40 data elements (*attributes*) and 10 decision classes if you have only 25 example decisions. Your application may learn the set of training examples with zero error, but all it is doing is storing each pattern exactly, without learning the correlations within the examples. If it were faced with a new set of attribute values, your application would have little ability to generalize and suggest correct decisions or predictions.

A good rule of thumb is that, for an application with N attributes and M decisions or predictions, you should use at least $10(M+N)$ examples for training. However, this is the minimum size for the training set. If you have plenty of data, it is better to use more data for training, as long as you leave enough to provide a test set of reasonable size. Common sense is required here to achieve a balance; the more data you use for training, the better the application should be, but the less test data you have available to see whether this is in fact the case.

Data Input Tool

Chapter 5.1

Overview

The Data Input tool brings data into Neural Connection from an external file and displays them as a spreadsheet. It allows you to:

• Specify the format of the data

• Choose the training, test, and validation set sizes

• Set the uses of individual fields in the data

• Randomize time series data for use with the Time Series window

• Manually edit entries in the data

The Data Input tool behaves as a separate program rather than as a dialog box. This means that it does not need to be closed before other actions take place on the workspace, and it can be resized and moved as if it were a standard Windows program window.

For more information on the format that data must be in before input into the Data Input tool and on training, test, and validation data, see Chapter 5, Input Tools.

This chapter provides the following information:

• Gives an overview of why the Data Input tool is useful

• Explains how to use the Data Input tool to import data into Neural Connection

• Explains how to select the format and usage of fields and data in the Data Input tool

• Shows how to specify the records that are to be used for training, validation, and testing

- Explains how to edit data and save your changes

- Explains how to use the Data Input tool to randomize time series data

Why Use the Data Input Tool?

The Data Input tool allows you to manipulate the input data directly in a transparent way and also allows a degree of freedom in specifying the usage of individual records and fields within the data. And if you are familiar with spreadsheets, it gives you the ability to import data into Neural Connection in a way with which you are already familiar.

A spreadsheet is a good way to display and manipulate data. In a spreadsheet, fields are represented by columns of data and records are represented by rows of data. A cell, the intersection of a row and a column, is the smallest element in a spreadsheet and contains an entry for a particular field in a particular record. Individual cells and groups of cells can be selected and edited, as can individual records and fields.

The Data Input tool uses letters and color codes to indicate features of the fields and records in your data; they are described below.

Data Sets

These codes appear on the screen in the second column from the left. They are listed below:

T = Training data, in cyan

X = Test data, in yellow

V = Validation data, in bright green

R = Run data, in pale blue

Field Usage

The codes listed below appear in the top row on the screen:

I = Input fields, in cyan

T = Target fields, in yellow

R = Reference fields, in bright green. These are passed through the application to be displayed on output but are not used or changed.

* = Unused fields. These are not passed through the application.

Other Color Codes

- *Inconsistent values* are marked in dark green. Inconsistencies include text in integer fields, previously unknown symbols, and similar conflicts. The field types are decided from the first 10 records in the training data, which are assumed to be correct and complete.

- *Missing values* are marked in bright blue.

- *Replacement values* for previously missing values are shown in light blue.

- *Encoded values* for previously missing values are shown in dark blue.

- *Out of range values* are shown in red.

- *Records with missing or inconsistent fields* are marked 1 on red in the left-most column.

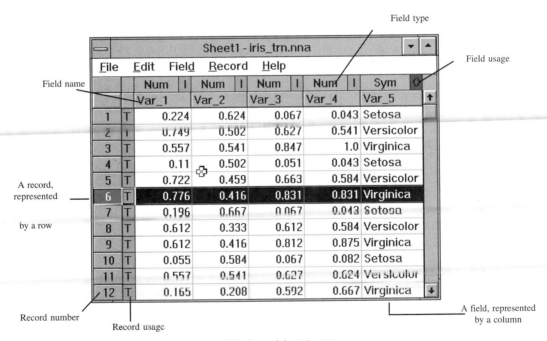

The Spreadsheet Input

Importing Data

Loading new development data resets your application and loses any training you have done.

To import your development data from an external file:

1. From the Data Input menu, choose **View**.

2. From the File menu, choose **Open**.

3. Select **Flat File**.

4. For the development data set, click **Configure**. Neural Connection then asks for a filename for your data file.

5. Select the data file that you want to import.

6. If your data file is a field count data (*.nna*) file, Neural Connection asks for the number of fields that the file contains. You must type this before the data file can be imported.

7. Click **OK**.

When data are imported into the Data Input tool, they are automatically parsed, each field is checked for consistency of data type, and the ranges of the field are calculated. If a discrepancy is found in the file that you have loaded, the record is marked as invalid and the erroneous cell is highlighted.

You can load separate run data without resetting the application.

To import your run data from an external file:

1. From the Data Input menu, choose **View**.

2. From the File menu, choose **Open**.

3. Select **Flat File**.

4. For the run data set, click **Configure**. Neural Connection then asks for a filename for your data file.

5. Select the data file that you want to import.

6. Click **OK**.

Fields

Field Configuration

Once the data set is open, you can set configuration parameters.

To select the configuration parameters:

- From the Field menu, choose **Configuration**.

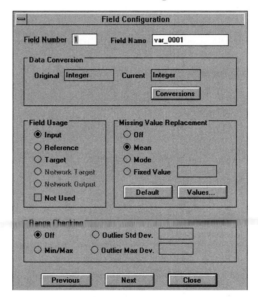

Field Configuration dialog box

Once the Field Configuration dialog box is open, you can:

- Move between fields
- Convert field formats
- Change field usage
- Check ranges
- Check missing values

Moving between Fields

To move between fields, in the Field Configuration dialog box:

• Click the **Next** or **Previous** buttons.

Field Usage

A field can be designated as one of the following:

• Input data

• Target data

• Reference data, which is passed but not used

• Not to be used,which is not passed through the application

You can change the usage either by using the Field Configuration dialog box or by clicking on the field usage code in the Data Input window.

To change the field usage using the Field Configuration dialog box:

1. From the Data Input menu, choose **View**.

2. From the Field menu, choose **Configuration**.

3. Select the field you want to change using the **Next** and **Previous** buttons.

4. Select the Field Usage you want.

5. Click **Close**.

To change the field usage from the Data Input window:

1. From the Data Input menu, choose **View**.

2. To open the Change field usage dialog box, click the top row.

3. Select the new field usage.

4. Click **OK**.

Change field usage dialog box

Ranges

The range checking options allow you to set up the parameters for recalculations. Range checking options include:

- No checking

- Checking for values outside the minimum and maximum range

- Checking for outliers

Range options are selected per field and calculated only if selected.

Minimum and maximum are calculated from the development data. When the deployment data set is run, values outside the range for a field are highlighted in red in the spreadsheet and in the left-most column. Maximum and minimum values are not highlighted on the development data.

The Outlier Standard Deviation and Outlier Maximum Deviation are calculated on the development data set. Any values outside the calculated standard and maximum deviation are highlighted on the spreadsheet. Outlier Standard Deviation defaults to 3. Outlier Maximum Deviation defaults to 5.

*Note: If you want to use test data in the calculation, set this by choosing **Allocation** in the Data menu. Click **Use test data** and then **Recalculate**.*

Since the settings for each field are used for both the development and deployment data, their formats must be the same if range checking is used.

To set range checking:

1. From the Data Input menu, choose **View**.

2. From the Field menu, choose **Configuration**.

3. Select the field you want to change using the **Next** and **Previous** buttons.

4. Check the Range Check option you require for the field.

5. Click **Close** and confirm the change.

Missing Values

These parameters specify how missing values are dealt with. Missing values in the data set may be:

- Encoded

- Replaced by a fixed value

- Replaced by the mean or mode values (symbolic fields are replaced by the mode)

- Left blank (- appears on the spreadsheet)

To search for missing values in the data set, choose **Statistics** from the Field menu.

To specify how the missing values are dealt with:

1. From the Data Input menu, choose **View**.

2. From the Field menu, choose **Configuration**.

3. Select the field you want to change using the **Next** and **Previous** buttons.

4. Check the Missing Values option you require for that field.

5. Click **Close** and confirm the change.

If you set an inappropriate Missing Values option, you can click **Default** to reset to the default. The default is that empty fields are replaced by the mean, or the mode for symbolic values, as specified in the Field Configuration dialog box. You may want to set up particular values in your data to reflect missing data with meaning. For example, you may want to code particular values as:

- *missing - irrelevant*, e.g., no credit card limit because no credit card

- *missing - unknown*, e.g., information not given

To set up encoding or to replace non-empty values:

1. From the Data Input menu, choose **View**.

2. From the Field menu, choose **Configuration**.

3. Select the field you want to change using the **Next** and **Previous** buttons.

4. In the Missing Value Replacement group, select **Values**. The Missing Values dialog box opens.

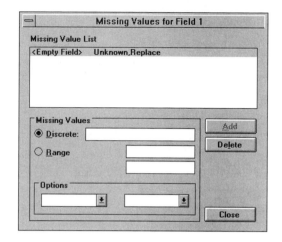

Missing Values dialog box

5. Either click **Discrete** and type a discrete value, or click **Range** and type a range of values to be replaced or encoded for this field.

6. In the Options group, from the left drop-down list select **Missing** or **Irrelevant**.

7. In the Options group, from the right drop-down list select **Replace** or **Encode**.

8. To add to the Missing Value list, click **Add**. To delete items from the Missing Value list, highlight them and click **Delete**.

9. Click **Close.**

Example

In the dialog box below, missing values have been set for field 4 in a data set. Empty fields will be replaced, but a 0 in the field will be encoded as irrelevant.

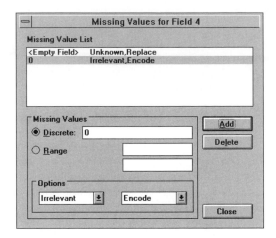

Example of Missing Values dialog box

In the Data Input window below, the value for the empty field has been replaced by the mean, **-4**, and the field with 0 in it has been encoded as **0(u)(i)**. You can also see examples of inconsistent fields setting the left-most column to **I**.

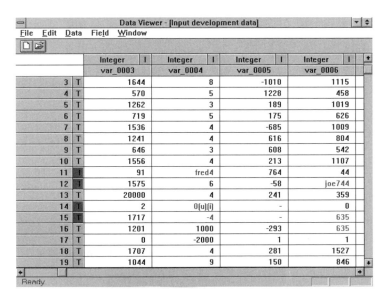

		Integer I	Integer I	Integer I	Integer I
		var_0003	var_0004	var_0005	var_0006
3	T	1644	8	-1010	1115
4	T	570	5	1228	458
5	T	1262	3	189	1019
6	T	719	5	175	626
7	T	1536	4	-685	1009
8	T	1241	4	616	804
9	T	646	3	608	542
10	T	1556	4	213	1107
11	I	91	fred4	764	44
12	I	1575	6	-58	joe744
13	T	20000	4	241	359
14	I	2	0(u)(i)	-	0
15	I	1717	-4	-	635
16	T	1201	1000	-293	635
17	T	0	-2000	1	1
18	T	1707	4	281	1527
19	T	1044	9	150	846

Example of Data Input window

Field Conversion

Once the data set is open, you can change the field type (integer, date, etc.).

To convert fields:

1. From the Data Input menu, choose **View**.

2. Click the Field Type cell above the field you want to change.

3. Select the field to be converted, using the **Previous** and **Next** buttons.

4. Select the conversion type from the list.

5. When the confirmation alert asks if you want to make the change, click **Yes**.

6. Click **Close**.

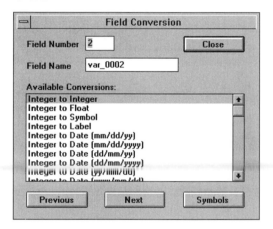

Field Conversion dialog box

When you convert a field from, or to, a symbolic field, you must tell the system how to convert the symbol.

To convert symbols:

1. From the Data Input menu, choose **View**.

2. Click the Field Type cell above the field you want to change.

3. Select the field to be converted, using the **Previous** and **Next** buttons.

4. In the Field Conversion dialog box, click **Symbols**.

5. Set the ranges for each symbol.

6. When the confirmation alert asks if you want to make the change, click **Yes**.

7. Click **Close**.

Class Equalization

When training an application it is necessary to use a data set that has roughly equal numbers of records in each class.

To generate an equalized data set:

1. From the Data Input menu, choose **View**.

2. From the Field menu, choose **Equalization**. The Choose field dialog box opens.

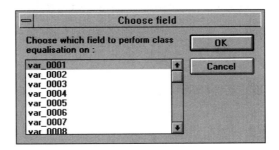

Choose field dialog box

3. Select the field to be equalized, and click **OK**. The Class Equalization dialog box opens.

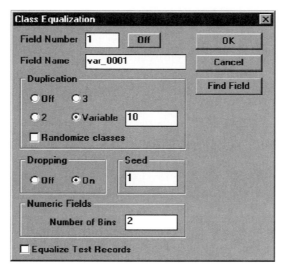

Class Equalization dialog box

There are several options for equalizing the data set. Records can be dropped, reducing the larger class; records can be duplicated, increasing the lowest classes; or a combination of techniques can be used.

To drop records:

1. In the Dropping group, click **On**.

2. Click **OK**.

The dropping will be done randomly. Change the value in the Seed field if another random number seed is to be used instead of the default value, 1.

To duplicate records:

1. In the Duplication group, click the button that corresponds to the maximum number of times that the records in the smaller class are to be duplicated. For example, if the "2" radio button is selected, then any particular record in the smaller group can be duplicated only twice, even if this means that the training will not be exactly balanced.

2. Click **OK**.

To equalize the test data set:

1. Select **Equalize Test Records**.

2. Click **OK**.

Statistics

The Field Statistics dialog box displays the range information for a variable. It is also used to check any inconsistencies.

Field Statistics dialog box

Note: Field statistics are available only for development data sets.

To look at statistics:

1. From the Data Input menu, choose **View**.

2. From the Field menu, choose **Statistics**.

Information provided includes:

*   Minimum value

*   Maximum value

*   Mean or mode value

*   The presence of missing values

*   The presence of inconsistent values

Fields with missing or inconsistent values have the **Missing Values** or **Inconsistent Values** boxes checked.

Field Statistics dialog box with Inconsistent Values selected

Where missing or inconsistent values are present, you can search for them by clicking **Search for...**. This opens the Missing Values dialog box.

Missing Values dialog box

This dialog box lists the record numbers with missing or inconsistent values for the field. The missing or inconsistent fields are also highlighted on the Data Viewer window in the spreadsheet and in the left-most column.

To find a particular record with missing values:

1. Highlight the missing value list.

2. Click **Find**.

To set up the way you want to deal with missing and inconsistent values, choose **Configuration** from the Field menu.

Field Name

The name of a field can be changed.

To change the name of a field:

1. From the Data Input menu, choose **View**.

2. Click the name of the field you want to change.

3. Type the desired name in the field provided.

4. Click **OK**.

Records

Record Usage

The use of individual records in the data file that you have imported can be specified in four ways:

Training data: The record will be used to train your application.

Validation data: The record will be used to validate the performance of your application during training.

Test data: The record will not be used in training; it will be used to generate a result when your application is run.

Not used: The record will not be used during training or running your application.

For more information on training, test, and validation data, see Chapter 5, Input Tools.

The use of records can be set individually or for the whole file.

Changing the Data Set

To change the data set:

1. From the Data Input menu, choose **View**.

2. Click the data set (the left-most column) to open the Change data set dialog box.

3. Select the new data set.

4. Click **OK**.

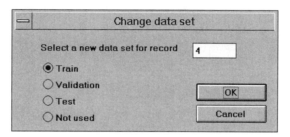

Change data set dialog box

Data Allocation

Once the data set is open, you can specify the order of the data and the records to be used for the training, validation, and test data sets.

To select the data set and data order:

1. From the Data Input menu, choose **View**.

2. From the Data menu, choose **Allocation**. This opens the development Data Allocation dialog box.

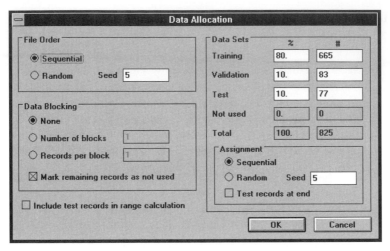

Data Allocation dialog box

This dialog box is used to select how records in a development data set are to be allocated for training, validation, and testing. The main functions available are:

- File order   Records can be selected sequentially or randomly using a specified seed.

- Data blocking   Records can be selected in blocks, with a specified number of records per block. If records are unused, they can be marked as such. Blocks can be selected sequentially or randomly.

- Data sets   The relative sizes of each data set for training, validation, and testing are set as percentages of the total. Normally, records are selected for training, validation, and test in that order. However, a random order can be selected.

When the relative sizes of the data sets are set up, the **Not used** row automatically calculates the number of records unused and sets the use of those records accordingly. If you set up more records than exist in the data set, the **Total** row displays the total in red.

When modeling time series data, it is important to select a test set that is at the end of the data set; that way, it contains the most recently recorded records.

To position the test data set at the end of the data file:

1. From the Data Input menu, choose **View**.

2. From the Data menu, choose **Allocation**.

3. In the Data Allocation dialog box's Assignment group, click **Test records at end**.

4. Click **OK**.

Randomizing Your Data Set

Note: *If you are performing time series analysis, read the section on time series analysis later in this chapter.*

The Data Input tool allows you to choose two methods for ordering your records within the data set:

File Order, Sequential: The data set is used in the order that it has when imported.

File Order, Random: The data set is randomized.

It is often useful to randomize the order of the data in the training file. There are two reasons for doing this:

- The validation data set chosen by Neural Connection is taken from the data immediately after the end of the training data. If the data have been collected so that there is an ordering in the data—for example, if all of class 1 are found at the beginning of the file and all of class 2 at the end of the file—the application would be trained on class 1 examples but validated on class 2 examples. This would lead to a solution that was not representative of the whole problem.

  Ideally, the training, validation, and test files should all contain data that represent the range of the entire problem.

- Some neural techniques are sensitive to the order in which data are presented to them. If they start to train primarily on class 1 examples, or on data in a specific range, they cannot easily compensate later for this initial bias.

Because of the possibility of hidden order correlations in your data, it is always wise to randomize the training file data. If you are undertaking time series analysis, more care needs to be taken in order not to destroy through-time correlations.

To select the data set record ordering technique:

1. From the Data Input menu, choose **View**.

2. From the Data menu, choose **Allocation**.

3. In the File Order group, select the required record ordering technique.

4. Click **OK**.

In order to allow you to repeat experiments exactly, a random number seed is provided for random ordering.

To set the random number seed:

1. From the Data Input menu, choose **View**.

2. From the Data menu, choose **Allocation**.

3. In the File Order group's **Seed** field, type the desired seed.

4. Click **OK**.

Time Series Analysis

Validation Data

One problem that often arises with time series analysis is how to validate the performance of the model that you develop. Conventionally, a validation set is used to check performance during training, and the data in the validation and training sets are randomized to ensure that both sets contain a representative sample of the data in the problem. However, in time series analysis, randomizing the data in this crude way would destroy the time history relationships that make time series analysis such a powerful tool.

To circumvent this difficulty, Data Input permits two alternate methods of validation set assignment: selection by random assignment and selection by blocks. Both of these allow selection effectively to take place *after* the time series windows have been generated by the Time Series window.

Selection by random assignment randomizes the selection of validation data throughout the time series. A random number seed is provided to allow the repetition of experiments. When this option is chosen, an individual time series record, or window, is used as training, test, or validation data according to the assignment of the first logical value in the window.

Selection in blocks divides the time series into a number of equal blocks, from the end of each of which is taken a validation set.

In each case, the total validation set size is determined by the value in the Data Sets group's **Validation %** field.

Note: *When using either of these techniques, you must ensure that the test records are positioned at the end of the file. This is necessary to limit the number of occasions when an individual piece of time information is present in both training and test data sets. If this is not done, then results may degrade.*

To select validation data randomly:

1. From the Data Input menu, choose **View**.

2. From the Data menu, choose **Allocation**.

3. Choose the **Random** option, and type a random number seed in the Assignment group.

4. Click **OK**.

To select validation data by blocks:

1. From the Data Input menu, choose **View**.

2. From the Data menu, choose **Allocation**.

3. In the Data Blocking group, select **Number of blocks**.

4. In the **Number of blocks** field, type the number of blocks required.

5. Click **OK**.

Editing Data

Editing Your Data Online

You can use the Data Input tool to edit an entry in your data.

To edit a record:

1. From the Data Input menu, choose **View**.

2. Highlight an entry in a record by selecting the desired cell. An edit cell appears on the title bar.

3. Edit the record.

4. Either accept the new entry by clicking the check button, or reject it by clicking the X button.

The record that is edited will automatically be parsed when it is accepted.

After you have made changes, you can save the data file from the Data Input tool.

To save the data file:

1. From the Data Input menu, choose **View**.

2. From the File menu, choose **Save**.

3. In the **File Name** field, type a name for the data file.

4. Click **OK**.

Saved Settings

As explained in Appendix I, a Neural Connection application is saved as a text file with an *.nni* extension. Within the file, each tool has its own text commands that set up the tool when it is loaded into Neural Connection. Some of these can be altered in text form, but it is strongly recommended that any changes be made using Neural Connection's workspace.

The application can be loaded into Neural Connection by using the **Open** command on the File menu.

An example of a saved Data Input tool text file is shown below:

```
[Spreadsheet Input]
.Name=Input1
.GridX=9
.GridY=14
{DEVELOPMENT DATA SOURCE}
{DATA SOURCE}
{FLATFILE}
FileName=D:\NCON2\IRISDATA.CSV
FileType=CommaSeparatedVariable
ColumnDelimiter=,
RecordDelimiter=<CR><LF>
RandomAccess=False
UseTextQuotes=False
{DATA INTERFACE}
NumColumns=5
NumRecords=150
InterfaceType=FlatFile
```

```
DataAccess=ReadOnly
FormatValid=True
Column000=var_0001,20,F,RW,Data
Column001=var_0002,20,F,RW,Data
Column002=var_0003,20,F,RW,Data
Column003=var_0004,20,F,RW,Data
Column004=var_0005,20,S,RW,Data
{DEPLOYMENT DATA SOURCE}
{DATA SOURCE}
{DATA SOURCE PRE-PROCESSOR}
FileOrderRandomise=False
FileOrderRandomSeed=5
DataBlocking=None
NumDataBlocks=1
RecordsPerBlock=1
RemainingNotUsed=True
DataSetRandomise=False
DataSetRandomSeed=5
PercentTrainRecords=80.000000
PercentValidationRecords=10.000000
PercentTestRecords=10.000000
PercentNotUsedRecords=0.000000
NumTrainRecords=0
NumValidationRecords=0
NumTestRecords=0
NumNotUsedRecords=0
MinTrainRecords=10
MaxTrainRecords=10000
TrainDataOffset=0
TestRecordsAtEnd=False
AllocateByPercent=True
{DATA SOURCE PROCESSOR}
SourcesIdentical=True
ExpandSymbols=False
TestRecordsInRanges=False
DuplicateRecords=10
DropRecords=True
EqualiseRandomSeed=1
EqualiseField=Off
EqualiseTestRecords=False
RandomiseClasses=False
EqualiseNumBins=2
UpdateRanges=False
RangeCalcRecords=500
RestrictRangeCalc=False
{DEVELOPMENT VECTOR DATA FORMAT}
FormatValid=True
NumFields=5
VectorFormat0000=var_0001,20,F,,UI,1,Me,O,F,F,F,
0.4333407383550096359,0,1,0.23210905522489216901
```

```
VectorFormat0001=var_0002,20,F,,UI,1,Me,O,F,F,F,
0.44451851546764376,0,1,0.18623804484234879331
VectorFormat0002=var_0003,20,F,,UI,1,Me,O,F,F,F,
0.46902962358737432247,0,1,0.30041875490223696188
VectorFormat0003=var_0004,20,F,,UI,1,Me,O,F,F,F,
0.4547407372958130467,0,1,0.31652185840059815503
VectorFormat0004=var_0005,20,S,,UT,1,Mo,O,F,F,F,0
Symbols:Setosa,0,0,Versicolour,0,0,Virginica,0,0
{END}
```

Output Tools

Chapter 6

Overview

Output tools provide the mechanisms for producing results from your application. Neural Connection has five output tools:

- Data Output, discussed in Chapter 6.1

- Text Output, discussed in Chapter 6.2

- Graphics Output, discussed in Chapter 6.3

- The What If? tool, discussed in Chapter 6.4

- The Time Series Plot, discussed in Chapter 6.5

Data Output Tool

Chapter 6.1

Overview

The Data Output tool runs topologies and either prints the results to the screen as a spreadsheet or saves them to a file.

The Data Output tool behaves as a separate program rather than as a dialog box. This means that it does not need to be closed before other actions take place on the workspace, and it can be resized and moved as if it were a standard Windows program window.

This chapter provides the following information:

- Gives an overview of the Data Output tool

- Explains how to run applications using the Data Output tool

- Explains how to customize the Data Output format

Why Use the Data Output Tool?

Use the Data Output Tool to:

- View a data set that has been passed through the application.

- Examine the results.

- Save the results in a file, or export them to another application.

The data are shown and manipulated in the Output Data Viewer window.

The Data Output tool has one significant difference from the Text Output tool: it can display and save run data, as well as training, validation, and test data.

Data Sets

The data sets are identified by the following colored codes in the left hand column on the screen:

T = Training data, in cyan

V = Validation data, in bright green

X = Test data, in yellow

R = Run data, in pale blue

Field Usage

The fields within data sets are identified by the following colored codes in the top row on the screen:

I = Input fields, in blue

T = Target fields, in yellow

R = Reference fields, in green

* = Unused fields

M = Network Target fields, in pale blue, are named *MTARGET1*, *MTARGET2*, etc.

O = Network Output fields, in pale green, are named *OUTPUT1*, *OUTPUT2*, etc.

Viewing Your Results in the Data Output Tool

If the application that you have built has not been trained, viewing the data set forces training to take place.

In order to view your results you must open the Output Data Viewer window.

To view your results:

1. From the Data Output menu, choose **View**.

2. From the View menu, choose the dataset that you want to view.

Scroll bars are provided to move around the text display if your results do not all fit in the window.

 To return to the workspace:

•   From the File menu, choose **Exit & Return**.

Saving Your Results

Results from Data Output can be directed to the screen or to a named file. Directing the results to a file saves them. Before you can save to a file, you must specify the name and path of the file you want to use.

To specify the output file name:

1. From the Data Output menu, choose **View**.

2. From the File menu, choose **Setup**.

3. Select **Flat-file** for the development or run data.

4. Select the appropriate **Configure** button.

5. In the Save As window, type the name and the file type.

6. In the Save As window, click **OK**.

7. In the Data Output window, click **Close**.

Note: *The development data and run data outputs are set up separately. When you are setting up the development data output, you must specify which development data set you want to output, using the radio buttons in the Data Output window.*

To save to a file from the Data Output tool:

1. From the Data Output menu, choose **View**.

2. Select **Output Development Data** or **Output Run Data**. Neural Connection asks you to confirm that you want to output the specified file.

3. Click **Yes**.

Note: *The development data written out is the data set that was specified by the* **Setup** *command. It is not necessarily the data set that is currently displayed.*

Customizing the Output

The results written out by your application and shown by the Data Output tool can be displayed in different ways.

You can customize the Data Output format by:

*   Choosing the fields you want to write out

*   Expanding symbolic output data

Selecting the Fields to Be Saved

By default the Data Output tool saves all the fields in the data set. However, it is possible to specify that a field not be saved.

To set a field so that it is not saved:

1. From the Data Output menu, choose **View**.

2. From the View menu, display a data set by selecting it.

3. Click the field usage cell at the top of the field that you do not want to save. The Change field usage dialog box displays.

Change field usage dialog box

4. In the Change field usage dialog box, set field usage to **Not Used**.

5. Click **OK**.

When this data is saved, any fields set to **Not Used** are not written out.

*Note: It is possible to set several fields to Not Used at once by putting a range of fields in the box **Select a new usage for field** in the Change field usage dialog box.*

Expanding Symbolic Outputs

If your target field and, therefore, your application output field are symbolic, you can choose to display or save the field in expanded form. This displays the 1-of-N encoding of the target and outputs.

1-of-N Encoding

This displays the target in a 1 or 0 format, with 0 being positive and all other possible classes having a value of 1. For example, in the Fisher Iris data, data that represented a Setosa would be displayed:

Setosa	Versicolor	Virginica
0.0	1.0	1.0

The outputs display as columns of values, with each column representing a possible decision. Neural Connection is designed to choose the lowest of the actual values as the correct decision. By comparing the actual values with the symbol value, you can see how sure your application is that the answer it has given is the correct answer. For example:

Setosa	Versicolor	Virginica
1.00008	0.41544	0.45448

Neural Connections's Iris application has made the decision *Versicolor*. You can see, however, that the application also had a low value for *Virginia*. This can point out possible problems in the future running of the application. This is particularly useful when the results are to be used as data in the future.

To expand symbolic outputs:

1. From the Data Output menu, choose **View**.

2. From the View menu, display a data set by selecting it.

3. From the Field menu, choose **Expand Symbols**.

Statistical Analysis

When a data file contains targets, it is useful to see how the application output compares to the targets over the range of the data. To do this, Neural Connection uses a *cross tabulation matrix*. A cross tabulation matrix is a table in which columns represent the class predicted by your application and rows represent the true class. If the results were 100% successful, the only entries would be along the leading diagonal of the matrix, and the sum of the diagonal entries would equal the number of examples in the data set. If the results were not 100% successful, misclassification errors would appear as off-diagonal entries.

To display the Cross Tabulation matrix:

1. From the Data Output menu, choose **View**.

2. From the View menu, display a data set by selecting it.

3. From the Field menu, choose **Cross Tabulation Matrix**.

4. If cross tabulations have not yet been calculated, Neural Connection asks you to confirm the calculation.

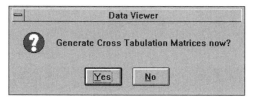

Confirm Cross Tabulation Matrices dialog box

5. Click **Yes**. This opens the Cross Tabulation Matrix dialog box.

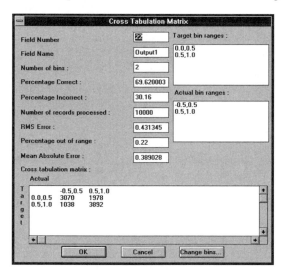

Cross Tabulation Matrix dialog box

To change the number of bins:

1. In the Cross Tabulation Matrix dialog box, click **Change Bins**. The Change bins dialog box appears.

2. Type a value in the **Number of bins** field.

3. Click **OK**. The Cross Tabulation Matrix dialog box reappears.

If the bins have been changed, you must run the application again to display the new cross tabulation matrix.

To re-run your application:

• From the View menu, choose a data set.

When you change the number of bins in a cross tabulation matrix, Neural Connection uses default bin ranges. These upper and lower values can be set independently for both the target bins and the application output, or *actual*, bins.

To set the bin values:

1. In the Cross Tabulation Matrix dialog box, click **Change Bins**. The Change bins dialog box appears.

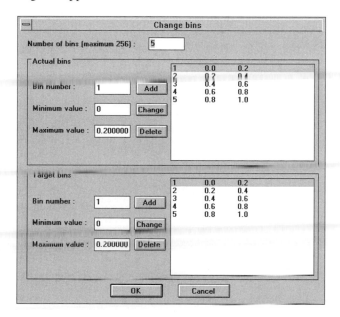

Change bins dialog box

2. Type a value in the **Number of bins** field.

3. To select the bin that you want to change, click the list in the Actual bins or Target bins group. This displays the details of the bin in the **Bin number**, **Minimum Value**, and **Maximum value** fields.

4. To change the maximum and minimum values, type them in the appropriate fields.

5. Click **Change**.

6. Click **OK**.

Note: *When you have loaded data you can reduce the time taken to perform operations by selecting **Ranges** from the Data menu, and calculating ranges over fewer records than are in the data set. However, this reduces the accuracy of some operations.*

Statistics

The **Statistics** command on the Window menu displays the statistics for the whole data set—for example, number of records.

To look at statistics:

• On the Window menu, click **Statistics**. This opens the Data Statistics dialog box.

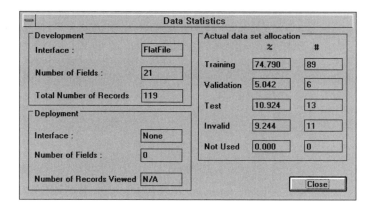

Data Statistics dialog box

Saved Settings

As explained in Appendix I, a Neural Connection application is saved as a text file with an *.nni* extension. Within the file, each tool has its own text commands that set up the tool when it is loaded into Neural Connection. Some of these can be altered in text form, but it is strongly recommended that any changes be made using Neural Connection's workspace.

The application can be loaded into Neural Connection by using the **Open** command on the File menu.

An example of a saved Data Output tool is shown below:

```
[Spreadsheet Output]
.Name=Output1
.GridX=24
.GridY=16
{DATA SOURCE PROCESSOR}
SourcesIdentical=True
ExpandSymbols=False
TestRecordsInRanges=False
DuplicateRecords=10
DropRecords=True
EqualiseRandomSeed=1
EqualiseField=Off
EqualiseTestRecords=False
RandomiseClasses=False
EqualiseNumBins=?
UpdateRanges=False
RangeCalcRecords=500
RestrictRangeCalc=False
{DEVELOPMENT VECTOR DATA FORMAT}
FormatValid=True
NumFields=22
VectorFormat0000=var_0001,20,I,,UI,1,Me,O,F,F,F,36,0,80,
23.592674447940758853
VectorFormat0001=var_0002,20,I,,UI,1,Me,O,F,F,F,840,0,1887,
539.22144614789954176
VectorFormat0002=var_0003,20,I,,UI,1,Me,O,F,F,F,4,0,10,
2.5114774726773516633
VectorFormat0003=var_0004,20,I,,UI,1,Me,O,F,F,F,-215,-
2000,1383,843.11209106586852613
VectorFormat0004=var_0005,20,I,,UI,1,Me,O,F,F,F,598,0,1743,
413.89758479427570137
VectorFormat0005=var_0006,20,I,,UI,1,Me,O,F,F,F,9,0,20,
6.9469546044439844934
VectorFormat0006=var_0007,20,I,,UI,1,Me,O,F,F,F,2,0,7,
1.4032509331378091311
VectorFormat0007=var_0008,20,I,,UI,1,Me,O,F,F,F,0,0,1,
0.45389251625762305764
```

```
VectorFormat0008=var_0009,20,I,,UI,1,Me,O,F,F,F,1,0,1,
0.49459279598483929519
VectorFormat0009=var_0010,20,S,,UI,1,Mo,O,F,F,F,1
Symbols:U,0,0,C,0,0,N,0,0,M,0,0
VectorFormat0010=var_0011,20,I,,UI,1,Me,O,F,F,F,0,0,1,
0.40171604172605818173
VectorFormat0011=var_0012,20,I,,UI,1,Me,O,F,F,F,0,0,1,
0.32211386229084282284
VectorFormat0012=var_0013,20,I,,UI,1,Me,O,F,F,F,0,0,1,
0.35448789495884408529
VectorFormat0013=var_0014,20,I,,UI,1,Me,O,F,F,F,0,0,1,
0.25605821339096562772
VectorFormat0014=var_0015,20,I,,UI,1,Me,O,F,F,F,0,0,1,
0.3125679070747381938
VectorFormat0015=var_0016,20,S,,UI,1,Mo,O,F,F,F,2
Symbols:B,0,0,C,0,0,J,0,0,G,0,0,F,0,0,
Symbols:E,0,0,D,0,0,U,0,0,K,0,0,I,0,0,
Symbols:A,0,0,H,0,0
VectorFormat0016=var_0017,20,S,,UI,1,Mo,O,F,F,F,0
Symbols:M,0,0,F,0,0,U,0,0
VectorFormat0017=var_0018,20,S,,UI,1,Mo,O,F,F,F,0
Symbols:M,0,0,O,0,0,U,0,0,S,0,0
VectorFormat0018=var_0019,20,S,,UI,1,Mo,O,F,F,F,1
Symbols:U,0,0,O,0,0,R,0,0,P,0,0
VectorFormat0019=var_0020,20,F,,UT,1,Me,O,F,F,F,
0.4945226917057902738,0,1,0.50036167079450322159
VectorFormat0020=MTarget1,20,F,,MT,1,Me,O,F,F,F,
0.4945226917057902738,0,1,0.50036167079450322159
VectorFormat0021=Output1,20,F,,MI,1,Me,O,F,F,F,
0.49801768973493054649,0.1206588745,1.090397358,
0.30826782394254276243
{DEVELOPMENT DATA SINK}
{DATA SINK}
{DEPLOYMENT DATA SINK}
{DATA SINK}
{DATA SINK PROCESSOR}
DataSet=Test
WriteMode=Overwrite
UpdateDataSinks=True
ViewDataSet=Test
ConfMtx21.NumBins=5
ConfMtx21.TargetBinRange0=0,0.200000003
ConfMtx21.TargetBinRange1=0.200000003,0.400000006
ConfMtx21.TargetBinRange2=0.400000006,0.6000000238
ConfMtx21.TargetBinRange3=0.6000000238,0.8000000119
ConfMtx21.TargetBinRange4=0.8000000119,1
ConfMtx21.ActualBinRange0=-0.1206588745,0.1215523705
ConfMtx21.ActualBinRange1=0.1215523705,0.3637636304
ConfMtx21.ActualBinRange2=0.3637636304,0.605974853
ConfMtx21.ActualBinRange3=0.605974853,0.8481861353
ConfMtx21.ActualBinRange4=0.8481861353,1.090397358
{END}
```

Text Output Tool

Chapter 6.2

Overview

The Text Output tool runs topologies and prints the results in text format, either to the screen or to a file.

This chapter provides the following information:

- Gives an overview of why text output is useful

- Explains how to run applications from the Text Output tool

- Explains how to customize the text output format

Why Use the Text Output Tool?

The Text Output tool gives results in a simple format that can be easily understood and gives straightforward guides to an application's performance.

Results produced as a data file can be passed directly to any other application that can read an ASCII format input. The Text Output tool can also write files in SPSS (.*sav*) file format so that you can take output files directly to SPSS for Windows.

Results can also be printed, or copied to other Windows applications.

Running an Application from the Text Output Tool

To run an application from the Text Output tool:

- From the Output Tool menu, choose **Run**.

When you run your application, the results appear in the format shown below. Columns are given headings so that they can be readily identified.

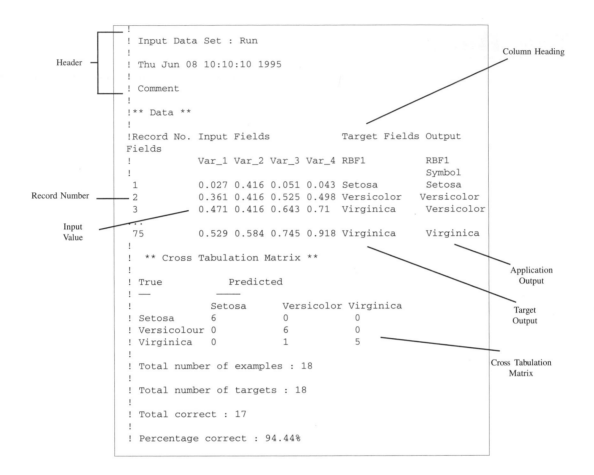

```
!
! Input Data Set : Run
!
! Thu Jun 08 10:10:10 1995
!
! Comment
!
!** Data **
!
!Record No. Input Fields          Target Fields Output
Fields
!          Var_1 Var_2 Var_3 Var_4 RBF1        RBF1
!                                               Symbol
 1          0.027 0.416 0.051 0.043 Setosa      Setosa
 2          0.361 0.416 0.525 0.498 Versicolor  Versicolor
 3          0.471 0.416 0.643 0.71  Virginica   Versicolor
...
 75         0.529 0.584 0.745 0.918 Virginica   Virginica
!
!  ** Cross Tabulation Matrix **
!
! True          Predicted
! ─            ────
!         Setosa     Versicolor Virginica
! Setosa     6          0          0
! Versicolour 0         6          0
! Virginica   0         1          5
!
! Total number of examples : 18
!
! Total number of targets : 18
!
! Total correct : 17
!
! Percentage correct : 94.44%
```

Header

Record Number

Input
Value

Column Heading

Application
Output

Target
Output

Cross Tabulation
Matrix

Text Output tool results

Scroll bars are provided to move around the text display if your results do not all fit in the window.

To return to the workspace:

• On the menu bar, click **Text Display Off!**.

Saving Your Results

Results from the Text Output tool can be directed to the screen or to a file. Directing the results to a file saves them.

To save output to a file:

1. From the Text Output menu, choose **Dialog**. The Data Output dialog box displays.

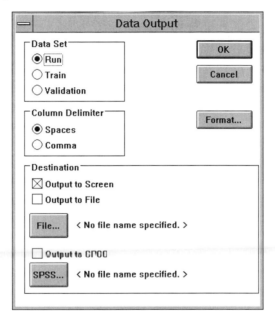

Data Output dialog box

2. In the **Destination** group, select the output destination required.

You can choose to save to the screen and to a file separately or at the same time, or you can choose to do neither. If you choose to save output to a file, you can specify the filename and path. If you do not, the file is saved as *results.nno*.

To specify the output file name:

1. From the Text Output menu, choose **Dialog**.

2. Click **File**.

3. Type the filename into the selection box. Either select the directory to which you want to save the file, or type the full path into the selection box.

4. Click **OK**.

Saving Your Results as an SPSS file

Results from the Text Output tool can be directed to an SPSS file.

To save output to an SPSS file:

1. From the Text Output menu, choose **Dialog**.

2. In the Destination group, select **Output to SPSS**.

If you choose to save output to an SPSS file, you can specify the filename and path. If you do not, the file is saved as *results.sav*.

To specify the SPSS file name:

1. From the Text Output menu, choose **Dialog**.

2. Click **SPSS**.

3. Type the filename into the selection box. Either select the directory to which you want to save the file, or type the full path into the selection box.

4. Click **OK**.

Printing Your Results

If your computer is connected to a printer, you can print the results that the Text Output tool has produced.

To print your results:

1. From the Text Output menu, choose **Run**. The results appear on the screen.

2. From the File menu, choose **Print**.

Copying Your Results

The results that you have produced can be copied from the Text Output tool and pasted into other Windows applications.

To copy the results:

1. From the Text Output menu, choose **Run**. The results appear on the screen.

2. From the Edit menu, choose **Copy**.

3. You can now paste the results into another application.

Choosing the Data to Be Used

When you first run an application, the Text Output tool displays the results from the test, or run, data specified in the Input tool. If you want to check how well your application has performed during training or validation, you can change the data set that Text Output displays to the training or validation data set. The results from these data appear the next time your application is run.

To change the data set type:

1. From the Text Output menu, choose **Dialog**.

2. In the Data Set box, click the type of data set required.

3. Click **OK**.

Customizing the Output

The results produced by your application and shown by the Text Output tool can be displayed in different ways. The following aspects of the text output format can be customized:

- The header

- The records you choose to show

- The data record input format

- The output format

- Whether or not you display the associated statistics

Changing the Header

You can use the Header box in the Output Format dialog box to alter the header of the results.

To display the Output Format dialog box:

1. From the Text Output menu, choose **Dialog**.

2. Click **Format**. The Output Format dialog box appears.

```
Output Format                                    ☒

                        ┌─────────┐   ┌──────────┐
                        │   OK    │   │  Cancel  │
                        └─────────┘   └──────────┘

Check items to include in data output.
┌─Header──────────────────────────────────────────┐
│    ☑ Date                                         │
│                   ┌─────────────────────────────┐ │
│    ☑ Comment      │                             │ │
│                   └─────────────────────────────┘ │
└───────────────────────────────────────────────────┘
┌─Data Record Format───────────────────────────────┐
│    ☑ Record Number      ☑ Input Field             │
│    ☑ Target Answer       ☑ Network Outputs         │
└───────────────────────────────────────────────────┘
┌─Decision Output Field────────────────────────────┐
│    ☑ Symbol              ☐ Actual Values           │
│    ☐ 1-of-N Encoded      ☐ Probabilities           │
└───────────────────────────────────────────────────┘
┌─Output Type──────────────┐ ┌─Statistics──────────┐
│    ☑ Correct Answers     │ │  ☑ Cross Tab Matrix  │
│    ☑ Incorrect Answers   │ │         ┌───┐         │
│                          │ │  Bins : │ 5 │         │
└──────────────────────────┘ └─────────┴───┴─────────┘
```

Output Format dialog box

To display the date:

• In the Header group, click **Date**.

To display a comment:

1. In the Header group, click **Comment**.

2. Type your comment in the comment field. Comments must be no more than 50 characters long.

Selecting the Records That Are Displayed

When a data file for a classification problem contains *targets* (the correct answers), you can display the correct and incorrect answers separately.

To display answers separately:

- In the Output Type group, select either **Correct Answers** or **Incorrect Answers**.

You can choose to view neither or both types of output.

The Data Record Format

The *record number* is the number assigned to each logical line in the input data. You can customize it using the Data Record Format group.

To display the record number:

- Select **Record Number**.

To display the input field:

- Select **Input Field**.

To display the target answer:

- Select **Target Answer**.

Where there is no target answer (for example, when you are using your application to assess new or unseen data), the **Target Answer** option is not available.

To display your Network Outputs:

- Select **Network Outputs**.

Decision Output Format

Changing the Decision Output Format

You can customize the decision output format for your application and can show or hide different data.

Network Outputs

When you are solving a decision problem, the Network Outputs can appear in several different ways. The result can be displayed as an absolute decision (*symbol*, or *1-of-N encoded*), or as a measure of the actual values that are produced by the final level of the application (*actual values*, or *probabilities*). This may be important in judging how well your application is making decisions.

Symbol	This is the name or string that you have assigned to a particular decision value of your application. For example, in the Fisher Iris data, the symbols are *Setosa*, *Versicolor*, and *Virginica*.
1-of-N Encoded	This gives the decision in a 1 or 0 format, with 0 being a positive decision and all other possible results of the decision having the value 1. For example, again in the Fisher Iris data, a decision that the data represented a Setosa would be displayed;

Setosa	Versicolor	Virginica
0.0	1.0	1.0

This is particularly useful when the results are to be used as data in the future.

Actual Values	The actual value is the numerical result from the last level of the application you created. It appears as columns of values with each column representing a possible decision. Neural Connection is designed to choose the lowest of the actual values as the correct decision. By comparing the actual values with the symbol value, you can see how sure your application is that the answer it has given is the correct answer. For example, with the actual values

Setosa	Versicolor	Virginica
1.00008	0.41544	0.45448

the Iris application has made the decision *Versicolor*. We can see, however, that the application also had a low value for Virginia. This can indicate possible problems in the future running of the application.

Probabilities	The *probabilities* are a normalized and scaled representation of the actual values. They give an indication of how sure the application is that a particular decision is correct. The probabilities appear as columns of values; Neural Connection is designed to choose the lowest.

Note: *The probabilities are not mathematical probabilities. Since Neural Connection chooses the lowest value produced by a network, they are a measure of 1-P, where P is the mathematical probability.*

To select the Network Output that is displayed:

• In the Decision Output Field group, select the appropriate boxes.

Statistical Analysis

When a data file contains targets, it is useful to see how the application output compares to the targets over the range of the data. To do this, Neural Connection uses a *cross tabulation matrix*. A cross tabulation matrix is a table in which columns represent the class predicted by your application, and rows represent the true class. If the results were 100% successful, the only entries would be along the leading diagonal of the matrix, and the sum of the diagonal entries would equal the number of examples in the data set. If the results were not 100% successful, misclassification errors would appear as off-diagonal entries.

To display the cross tabulation matrix:

- In the Statistics group, select **Cross Tab Matrix**.

In decision problems the cross tabulation matrix is defined in terms of the symbols that you have assigned to the decisions. In prediction problems the matrix is defined in terms of small increments in value. For example, all the predictions or results within the values of 0.1 and 0.3, 0.3 and 0.5, 0.5 and 0.7, etc., can be viewed together. These small increments are called *bins*, and the number of bins used can be changed to alter the size of the increments, and therefore the definition of the matrix. You can choose to have between 1 and 20 bins in your cross tabulation matrix.

To change the number of bins:

- In the **Bins** field, type in the number of bins you require.

Saved Settings

As explained in Appendix I, a Neural Connection application is saved as a text file with an *.nni* extension. Within the file, each tool has its own text commands that set up the tool when it is loaded into Neural Connection. Some of these can be altered in text form, but it is strongly recommended that any changes be made using Neural Connection's workspace.

The application can be loaded into Neural Connection by using the **Open** command on the File menu.

An example of a saved Text Output tool is given below:

```
[Text Output]
.Name=Text1
.GridX=24
```

```
.GridY=12
Version="1.0"
ProblemType=UNKNOWN
NumberOut=0
CalcErr=TRUE
DataSet=TEST
ToFile=FALSE
ToScreen=TRUE
OutputFile=""
DelimiterChar="Space"
Date=TRUE
Comment=TRUE
CommentText=""
RecordNum=TRUE
InputField=TRUE
TargetAns=TRUE
NetworkOutput=TRUE
Symbol=TRUE
ActualValues=FALSE
1OfN=FALSE
Prob=FALSE
CorrectAns=TRUE
IncorrectAns=TRUE
CrosstabMatrix=TRUE
Bins=5
```

Graphics Output Tool

Chapter 6.3

Overview

The Graphics Output tool runs applications and displays the results in the results window as a 3-D plot of the network output against two of the inputs. It functions only if a Simulator tool has been used in the application (see Chapter 8.3).

This chapter provides the following information:

- Gives an overview of the advantages of using graphical output

- Explains how to run an application from the Graphics Output tool

- Explains how to alter the resulting graph

*Note: The Graphics Output tool does not have a **Dialog…** box.*

Why Use the Graphics Output Tool?

The Graphics Output tool allows you to see how your application has modeled your problem across two of your input variables. This can give you an insight into the success of the model—has the application modeled the problem in the same way as you might expect? If it has, then your confidence in the model can be increased. If it hasn't, but it is still getting good results, perhaps there is some unintuitive or previously unknown trend in your data that needs to be examined.

The Graphics Output tool allows you to print your results, to save them as a Windows bitmap, or to copy them to other Windows applications.

Running an Application from the Graphics Output Tool

Before an application can be run from the Graphics Output tool, a Simulator tool must be placed in the correct position in the topology and correctly activated.

For further information see Chapter 8.3, Simulator Tool.

To run an application from the Graphics Output tool:

• From the Output Tool menu, choose **Run**.

When you run an application from the Graphics Output tool, a Graphics Display window opens and your graph appears in a wire mesh format from an automatically selected view point.

To return to the workspace:

• On the menu bar, click **Graphics Display Off!**.

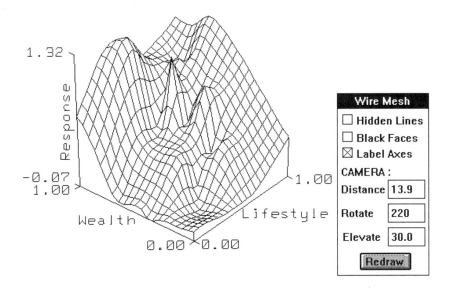

The Graphics Display window

Changing the Graphics Output Display

Changing the Inputs

The inputs that appear on the graph drawn by the Graphics Output tool must be selected in the Simulator tool that provides the Graphics Output with a simulated test set.

For further information see Chapter 8.3, Simulator Tool.

The axes of the graph are labeled with the inputs and output, and vary between the maxima and minima selected in the Simulator tool.

To display the axes labels:

1. In the Wire Mesh box, click **Label Axes**.

2. Click **Redraw**.

Hidden Lines

Where part of the graph is obscured by another part of the graph, the hidden lines can be drawn in.

To draw hidden lines:

1. In the Wire Mesh box, click **Hidden Lines**.

2. Click **Redraw**.

Opaque Faces

When part of the graph is viewed from behind an axis wall, the wall can be made opaque or transparent. Opaque walls are known as opaque faces.

To create opaque faces:

1. In the Wire Mesh box, click **Opaque Faces**.

2. Click **Redraw**.

Altering the Point of View

The camera position can be rotated horizontally or vertically to any position you require.

To alter the camera position:

1. In the Wire Mesh box's **Elevate** and **Rotate** fields, type the coordinates of the required point of view.

2. Click **Redraw**.

Saving Your Results

Results from **Graphics Output** can be directed to a file.   This saves the graph as a Windows bitmap.

To save to a file:

1. From the Graphics Output menu, choose **Run**.

2. From the File menu, choose **Print to File**.   A dialog box requests a name and path for the bitmap file. You must specify the name of the file before you can save the graph.

3. In the **File Name** text field, type the desired name.

4. Click **OK**.

Printing Your Results

If your computer is connected to a printer, you can print the results that the Graphics Output has produced.

To print your results:

1. From the Graphics Output menu, choose **Run**. The results appear on the screen.

2. From the File menu, choose **Print**.

Copying Your Results

The results that you have produced can be copied from the Graphics Output and pasted into other Windows applications.

To copy the results:

1. From the Graphics Output menu, choose **Run**. The results appear on the screen.

2. From the Edit menu, choose **Copy**.

You can now paste the results into another application.

Saved Settings

As explained in Appendix I, a Neural Connection application is saved as a text file with an *.nni* extension. Within the file, each tool has its own text commands that set up the tool when it is loaded into Neural Connection. Some of these can be altered in text form, but it is strongly recommended that any changes be made using Neural Connection's workspace.

The application can be loaded into Neural Connection by using the **Open** command on the File menu.

An example of a saved Graphics Output tool is shown below:

```
[Graphics Output]
.Name=Graph1
.GridX=26
.GridY=14
Version="1.0"
DataSet=TEST
ZAxis=0
NX=21
NY=21
DataLimits=0,1,0,1,0.12449061870574951172,
1.2552798986434936523,1,1,10,10,-5,-5
XLabel="RBF4"
YLabel="RBF5"
ZLabel="RBF6"
Ranges=1,0,1,0
HiddenLines=FALSE
BlackFaces=FALSE
LabelAxes=TRUE
Distance=13.800000000000000711
Rotation=220
Elevation=30
```

What If? Tool

Chapter 6.4

Overview

The What If? tool is a way of readily seeing the influence that changing one variable has on another. For example, if advertising increases by 2%, what will the effect be on sales? The What If? tool produces a visual output of the response of your application and allows you to produce a mathematical model of a specific area of the response.

This chapter provides the following information:

- Explains why the What If? tool is useful

- Explains how to use the What If? tool

*Note: The What If? tool does not have a **Dialog...** box.*

Why Use the What If? Tool?

If you have built a good model of your problem, it represents the interrelationships among input values in the real world. It is useful to be able to see the dependencies between pairs of these input values; by seeing how one value rises and falls when another changes, you can make better decisions.

The What If? tool simultaneously provides three different outputs:

- A sensitivity plot of the output response against two of the input variables

- A cross section of the sensitivity plot

- A text display showing the effect of changes in current conditions

Running an Application from the What If? Tool

Before an application can be run from the What If? output tool, a Simulator tool must be placed in the correct position in the topology and correctly activated. For further information see Chapter 8.3, Simulator Tool.

To run the What If? tool:

• From the What If? tool menu, choose **Run**. The What If... window appears.

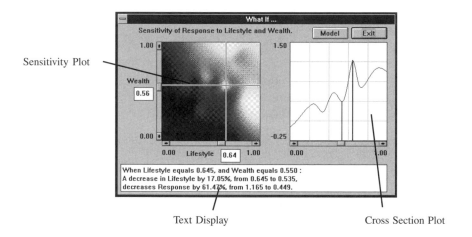

The What If... window

Note: *The What If? tool may take some time to run, due to the detail in the sensitivity plot. The time taken to run can be decreased by decreasing the number of values used in the Simulator Tool (see Chapter 8.3).*

To return to the workspace:

• Click **Exit**.

The What If... Window

On the left of the What If... window is the sensitivity plot of the output from the model against two inputs.

The output of the model is taken as two of the modeling tool's inputs are varied across their ranges. The initial points for the plot are taken at the resolution set in the Simulator Tool and further points are then interpolated between them up to a resolution of 200 x 200 points. The interpolation rule used is one of cubic spline interpolation.

Note: *When using low resolutions in the Simulator Tool, some features displayed on the sensitivity plot may be artifacts created by the interpolation technique.*

High output values are shown by light colors and low output values by dark colors. The names of the inputs being varied are shown on the edges of the plot.

Two movable axes are provided for the sensitivity plot. The horizontal axis determines the position of the cross section plot and the vertical axis determines the position of the blue 'origin' line on the cross section plot.

To move the horizontal axis of the sensitivity plot:

1. From the What If? tool menu, choose **Run**.

2. Do one of the following:

   - In the horizontal axis text edit field, to the left of the sensitivity plot, type the desired position of the cross section, and press **Enter.**

   or

   - Use the scroll bar to the left of the plot to move the cross section line.

To move the vertical axis of the sensitivity plot:

1. From the What If? tool menu, choose **Run**.

2. Do one of the following:

   - In the vertical axis text edit field, at the bottom of the sensitivity plot, type the desired position of the cross section, and press **Enter.**

   or

   - Use the scroll bar to the bottom of the Plot to move the cross section line.

On the right hand side of the What If… window is the cross section plot. This shows the cross section through the sensitivity plot at the horizontal axis.

The What If? tool uses the cross section plot to produce an analysis of how a change in one variable will affect the output. The blue *origin* line in the cross section represents the position of the vertical axis of the sensitivity plot. It provides the base point for the analysis of changes in the variable.

The red line in the cross section is the *change* line. By moving it along the cross section you produce a measure of the sensitivity of the output to the inputs you have chosen.

To move the red change line on the cross section plot:

1. From the What If? tool menu, choose **Run**.

2. Use the scroll bar beneath the cross section plot to move the change line.

The Text Display expresses in words the change in the output predicted by your model if a change in the variables represented by the sensitivity plot occurred, from the origin line to the change line.

Note: The What If? tool can produce a meaningful result only if you are examining an area of interest in your data. All of the input fields other than the two displayed in the sensitivity plot are held to fixed values during this analysis. The fixed values used are specified in the Simulator Tool (see Chapter 8.3).

Saved Settings

As explained in Appendix I, a Neural Connection application is saved as a text file with an *.nni* extension. Within the file, each tool has its own text commands that set up the tool when it is loaded into Neural Connection. Some of these can be altered in text form, but it is strongly recommended that any changes be made using Neural Connection's workspace.

The application can be loaded into Neural Connection by using the **Open** command on the File menu.

An example of a saved What If? tool is given below:

```
[What If]
.Name=WhatIf1
.GridX=26
.GridY=12
Version="1.0"
Ranges=1,0,1,0
NumX=0
NumY=0
NX=21
NY=21
LIMITS=0,1,0,1,-0.25,1.5
FIELD=0
DSet=TRAIN
SimID=0
DataSet=TEST
```

Time Series Plot

Chapter 6.5

Overview

Time Series Plot displays results from an application that it runs in a graphical form, as a 2-D plot against time.

This chapter provides the following information:

- Gives an overview of when the Time Series Plot is useful

- Explains how to run applications from the Time Series Plot tool

- Explains how to customize the graphical output

Why Use the Time Series Plot?

If your data are in the form of a time series, the relationship through time of the predicted result of a system and the actual result can give you a good idea of the performance of your model. The Time Series Plot gives you the ability to see how well your application is modeling the problem through time by visually comparing the actual outputs to either the target output or the inputs.

The graph produced by the Time Series Plot can be printed, saved as a bitmap file, or copied to another Windows application.

Running an Application from the Time Series Plot

To run an application from Time Series Plot:

- From the Time Series Plot menu, choose **Run**. A Graphics Display window opens, and your graph appears as a two dimensional plot.

Different types of data appear in different colors:

Data Type	Color
Application output	red
Target data, training data set	dark blue
Target data, validation data set	green
Target data, test data set	light blue
Input data	purple

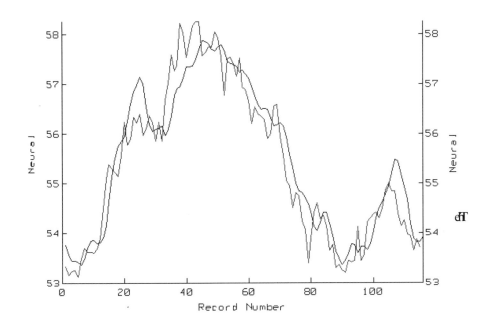

Time Series Plot output

To return to the workspace:

• On the menu bar, click **Graphics Display Off!**.

Customizing the Output

Choosing the Data to Be Used

When you first run an application, Time Series Plot displays the results from the test, or run, data specified in the file source. If you want to check how well your application has performed during training or validation, you can change the data set that Time Series Plot displays to the combined training and validation set. The results from these data appear the next time your application is run from the Time Series Plot.

To change the data set:

1. From the Time Series Plot menu, choose **Dialog**.

2. In the Data Set group, click the required data set.

3. Click **OK**.

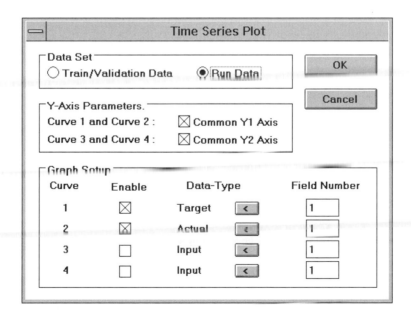

The Time Series Plot dialog window

Choosing Which Curves Are Plotted

Up to four curves can be plotted, two on one graph and two on a second graph. Each curve represents one value throughout the time period covered.

To view a curve:

1. From the Time Series Plot menu, choose **Dialog**.

2. Select the **Enable** box next to the curve you want to view.

3. Click **OK**.

Curves one and two are always displayed on the first graph and curves three and four on the second graph.

Each curve can represent either an input attribute, a target value, or an actual value (the application output). Where there is more than one value in these categories, you can select the element to use. For example, when there are four inputs, you can choose the first, second, third, or fourth element.

To select the value that a curve represents:

1. From the Time Series Plot menu, choose **Dialog**.

2. Use the < button to change the data type to the desired type.

3. In the **Field No.** field, type the desired element number.

4. Click **OK**.

Plot Axes

The *x* axis on the plot is fixed to the intervals used in the test and training data. The scale represents the number of records in the data.

The *y* axis represents the actual value of the element used. The left hand axis of the first plot refers to curve one and the right hand axis to curve two. The left hand axis of the second plot refers to curve three and the right hand axis to curve four. The *y* axis parameters of each graph can be fixed to the same scale.

To fix the *y* axis parameters:

1. From the Time Series Plot menu, choose **Dialog**.

2. To fix the *y* axes of the first plot, select **Common Y1 Axis**.

3. To fix the *y* axes of the second plot, select **Common Y2 Axis**.

4. Click **OK**.

Saving Your Results

You can direct the results from Time Series Plot to a file.   Doing so saves the graph as a Windows bitmap.

To save to a file:

From the Time Series Plot menu, choose **Run**.

1. From the File menu, choose **Print to File**. A dialog box appears requesting a name and path for the bitmap file. You must specify the name of the file before you can save the graph.

2. In the **File Name** text field, type the desired name.

3. Click **OK**.

Printing Your Results

If your computer is connected to a printer, you can print the results that the Time Series Plot produces.

To print your results:

1. From the Time Series Plot menu, choose **Run**. The results appear on the screen.

2. From the File menu, choose **Print**.

Copying Your Results

The results can be copied from the Time Series Plot and pasted into other Windows applications.

To copy the results:

1. From the Time Series Plot menu, choose **Run**. The results appear on the screen.

2. From the Edit menu, choose **Copy**.

You can now paste the results into another application.

Saved Settings

As explained in Appendix I, a Neural Connection application is saved as a text file with an *.nni* extension. Within the file, each tool has its own text commands that set up the tool when it is loaded into Neural Connection. Some of these can be altered in text form, but it is strongly recommended that any changes be made using Neural Connection's workspace.

The application can be loaded into Neural Connection by using the **Open** command on the File menu.

An example of a saved Time Series Plot tool is shown below:

```
[Time Series Plot]
.Name=TSP1
.GridX=18
.GridY=9
Version="1.0"
ICurve1=25,0,"Bayes1"
ICurve2=25,0,"Bayes1"
ICurve3=-1980475767,0,""
ICurve4=0,0,""
GotTargets=TRUE
GotActuals=TRUE
DataSet=TEST
CommonY1=TRUE
CommonY2=TRUE
Curve1=TRUE
VecType1="Target"
VecCol1=0
Curve2=TRUE
VecType2="Actual"
VecCol2=0
Curve3=FALSE
VecType3="Input"
VecCol3=0
Curve4=FALSE
VecType4="Input"
VecCol4=0
```

Modeling and Forecasting Tools

Chapter 7

Overview

Neural Connection has six modeling and forecasting tools. Three are neural computing techniques: the Multi-Layer Perceptron, Radial Basis Function, and Kohonen tool. Three are statistical techniques: Closest Class Mean Classifier, Regression tool, and Principal Component Analysis.

The tools and how to use them are detailed in the following chapters:

This chapter explains how model building enables you to solve complex problems.

Using Models to Solve Problems

Neural Connection uses a modeling approach to solving problems. The modeling and forecasting tools are the key elements in Neural Connection that allow you to do this. A good model covers the entire range of operation of a problem and is therefore able to cope with any inputs that are presented to it. By using current data to build a model of the relationships between inputs and outputs, we can readily predict new output values based on previously unseen inputs. Neural networks are particularly good at modeling complex problems and problems where the data are masked by noise.

Multi-Layer Perceptron

Chapter 7.1

Overview

The Multi-Layer Perceptron is a modeling and forecasting tool that uses a neural network to model your data. It can be used to classify patterns or to predict values from your data. Because it uses a supervised learning technique, it requires that your data contain targets for training the network.

This chapter provides the following information:

- Explains why the Multi-Layer Perceptron is useful

- Introduces the ideas behind the Multi-Layer Perceptron

- Explains how to train the Multi-Layer Perceptron to produce an output

- Explains how to improve the results produced by the Multi-Layer Perceptron

What Is a Multi-Layer Perceptron?

The Multi-Layer Perceptron is a neural network that is based on the original Simple Perceptron model (see below) but with additional hidden layers of neurons between the input and output layers. Multi-Layer Perceptrons are the most commonly used neural computing technique.

Why Use a Multi-Layer Perceptron?

Multi-Layer Perceptrons can produce good models that accurately represent nonlinearitics in your data.

Simple Perceptrons

A Perceptron consists of an input layer and an output layer. There are no hidden layers. Each neuron in the input layer is connected to each neuron in the output layer and these connections between the input and output layers are adjusted as the network is trained.

The output from any neuron in a Perceptron is the product of its inputs and a weighting. Given any input pattern, a Perceptron produces a set of output values that depends only on the input pattern and on the values of the connections.

Simple Perceptrons can solve linearly separable problems but there are many classes of problems that are linearly inseparable (including many real-world problems), which therefore cannot be solved by simple Perceptrons. In order to solve these more difficult problems, it is necessary to use the more powerful Multi-Layer Perceptrons.

Multi-Layer Perceptrons

A Multi-Layer Perceptron differs from the Simple Perceptron in two major ways.

First, it has an additional layer of neurons between the input and output layer, known as the *hidden* layer. This layer vastly increases the learning power of the Multi-Layer Perceptron.

Second, it uses a transfer, or activation, function to modify the input to a neuron.

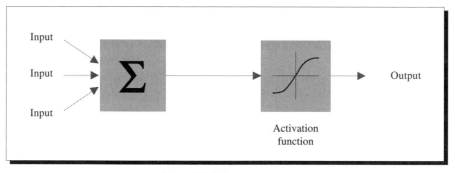

An artificial neuron

The activation of hidden and output layer neurons is the same as in the case of simple Perceptrons, while the transfer function is a smooth nonlinear function, usually the sigmoid function. This function is chosen because the algorithm requires a response function with a continuous, single-valued first derivative.

Training proceeds in the following way. First, the weights and biases in the network are initialized, usually to small random values. A training pattern is then applied to the input units and the activations of neurons in the first hidden layer are calculated. The outputs produced by these neurons via the transfer function are then fed to neurons in the following layer. This forward pass process is repeated at each layer until an output signal from neurons in the output layer is obtained.

The difference between the actual and desired output values is measured, and the network model connection strengths are changed so that the outputs produced by the network become closer to the desired outputs. This is achieved by a backward pass during which connection changes are propagated back through the network, starting with the connections to the output layer and ending with those to the input layer.

The basic recipe, the learning rule, for changing the connections is simple. If the output produced by the network is correct, the connections from the output neurons to all input neurons are unchanged. If the network's output is larger than the desired output at any node, then the connections between that neuron and all input neurons are decreased. If the outputs are smaller than desired, the connection values are increased.

There are two points worth noting about this learning process. First, the algorithm used is a gradient descent process that finds only the nearest local minimum in the mean square error from any given set of initial connection values. Because there are many minimums, there is almost certainly a better (i.e., lower mean square error) minimum corresponding to some other set of connections. It may be necessary to run the algorithm from many different starting values to find a good optimum. Second, the rate of convergence depends on the values chosen by the user for the learning rate and momentum.

Training

To train the Multi-Layer Perceptron:

- From the Multi-Layer Perceptron menu, choose **Train**.

Neural Connection displays the MLP Performance window during training.

When Neural Connection trains a Multi-Layer Perceptron, it uses an incremental learning technique whereby the Multi-Layer Perceptron is trained in stages. In the first stage, a sample of examples from the training set is used to train the Multi-Layer Perceptron. The best network produced at this stage is then passed to the second stage and is used as a starting point for training. In the second stage, a larger sample of the data is used to train the network, and, again, the best network is passed on to the next stage. This procedure continues for four stages.

Note: *The samples used in the training are taken sequentially, not randomly. This may give you poor results if the training set consists of ordered examples. To avoid this problem, randomize your training set.*

Neural Connection allows you to specify the maximum number of examples and the number of updates to be used in a training stage.

To change the number of updates or examples:

1. From the Multi-Layer Perceptron menu, choose **Dialog**. The Multi-Layer Perceptron Network dialog box displays.

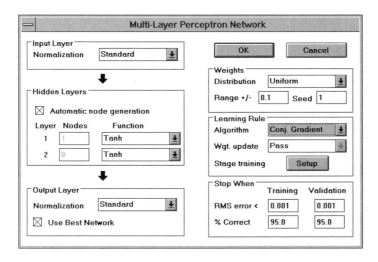

Multi-Layer Perceptron Network dialog box

2. In the Learning Rule group, click **Setup**. The Training Stages dialog box displays.

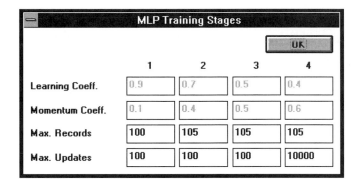

Training Stages dialog box

3. In the **Max. Updates** and **Max. Records** fields, type the number of updates and maximum number of records required.

4. Click **OK**.

Stopping Training

Training can be stopped at any time by clicking **STOP** in the Training Dialog Window. This may be necessary when the MLP is unable to find a global minimum error that satisfies the stopping criteria. When this occurs, the error plot in the Training Dialog Window usually approaches a flat line. However, this is not a guarantee that further training won't enable a global minimum to be reached.

To stop training:

1. In the MLP Performance window, click **STOP**.

2. Click **Exit**.

The Multi-Layer Perceptron stops training when one of the convergence criteria has been met. The convergence criteria appear in the Convergence group in the Dialog box.

For prediction problems, the RMS Error determines the optimum value of root mean square error in the validation and training data sets. For decision problems, the % Correct defines the percentage of examples that must be correctly classified for training to stop.

To change the convergence criteria:

1. From the Multi Layer Perceptron menu, choose **Dialog**.

2. In the **Stop When** group's fields, type the desired values.

3. Click **OK**.

Running Your Data

When you run your data through a trained Multi-Layer Perceptron, you can choose to use either the network that gave the best results during training or the final network that was used in training.

To choose the network:

1. From the Multi-Layer Perceptron menu, choose **Dialog**.

2. In the Output Layer group, select or deselect **Use Best Network**.

3. Click **OK**.

Improving Your Results

The decisions that affect the performance of your Multi-Layer Perceptron are:

- The number of hidden layers

- The number of nodes in each layer

- The transfer, or activation, function used by the nodes

- The learning algorithm used by the Multi-Layer Perceptron

- The initial values of the weights between nodes

The Number of Hidden Layers

In Neural Connection, Multi-Layer Perceptrons can have either one or two hidden layers. This can either be decided automatically, based on the data presented to the Multi-Layer Perceptron, or it can be set manually.

In most problems, a second hidden layer does not produce a large improvement in performance.

To choose the number of hidden layers:

1. From the Multi-Layer Perceptron menu, choose **Dialog**

2. In the Hidden Layers group, deselect **Automatic node generation**.

3. In the **Nodes** field of the layer(s) that you want to use, type a number of nodes (see below). If no nodes are specified, the layer will be disabled.

4. Click **OK**.

The Number of Nodes in Each Layer

The number of nodes in a layer can either be selected automatically by Neural Connection or it can be set independently. In most cases, increasing the number of nodes improves the performance of the Multi-Layer Perceptron on the training data but not necessarily on the validation data.

If you add enough hidden units, the network will get its training set 100% correct because it will have enough weights to represent exactly all of the training patterns. This would, however, be an extremely poor network, as it would have little ability to generalize or find solutions for examples that it had not been trained on.

The correct way of assessing the impact of the number of hidden units on a problem is to look at performance on the validation set. As the total number of hidden units is increased from one, the network performance on the validation data increases rapidly. This is because each new hidden unit starts to represent one of the underlying features in the data set.

As more units are added, performance levels off. Adding further units may then cause a decrease in performance because the power of generalization is lost and the network begins to learn the noise present in the data.

By using a measure of the error in the validation set as part of its convergence criteria, Neural Connection reduces the danger of over learning, but it is still best to use as few nodes as possible to achieve the desired result.

To set the number of nodes in a layer:

1. From the Multi-Layer Perceptron menu, choose **Dialog**.

2. In the Hidden Layers group, click to deselect **Automatic node generation**.

3. In the **Nodes** field of the appropriate layer, type the desired number of nodes.

4. Click **OK**.

The Node Activation Function

The type of activation functions used in a layer can either be selected automatically by Neural Connection or it can be set independently.

Neural Connection allows you to use tanh, sigmoid, or linear functions as the activation function. Choosing a different function may improve your results.

To choose the activation function used in a layer:

1. From the Multi-Layer Perceptron menu, choose **Dialog**.

2. In the Hidden Layers group, deselect **Automatic node generation**.

3. Click the **Function** drop-down list.

4. Click the desired activation function.

5. Click **OK**.

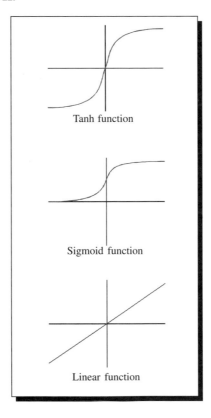

Tanh function

Sigmoid function

Linear function

The Learning Algorithm

The Multi-Layer Perceptron can use one of two algorithms to change the weights of the connections between nodes: conjugate gradient or steepest descent.

Conjugate Gradient

The *conjugate gradient* method measures the gradient of the error surface after each pass. It then alters the weights of the node inputs using a compromise between the direction of the steepest gradient and the previous direction of change.

Steepest Descent

The *steepest descent* method measures the gradient of the error surface after each iteration and changes the weights in the direction of the steepest gradient.

When a minimum is reached, a new gradient is measured and the weights are changed in the new direction. As each new gradient must necessarily be at right angles to the previous direction, this can be a crude technique. To improve the usefulness of the Steepest Descent method, two parameters can be altered: the momentum coefficient and the learning coefficient.

The *learning* coefficient weights the change in the connections. If it is too high, the learning algorithm will overshoot the minimum; if it is too low, the algorithm will take too long to reach the minimum. There is no hard and fast rule about what value the learning coefficient should have.

The *momentum* coefficient is a term that tends to alter the change in the connections in the direction of the average gradient. This can prevent the learning algorithm from stopping in a local minimum rather than the global (ideal) minimum.

To choose the learning algorithm:

1. From the Multi-Layer Perceptron menu, choose **Dialog**.

2. In the Learning Rule group, click the **Algorithm** drop-down list.

3. Click the desired learning algorithm.

4. Click **OK**.

To alter the learning and momentum coefficients:

1. From the Multi-Layer Perceptron menu, choose **Dialog**.

2. In the Learning Rule group, click **Setup**.

3. In the Training Stages window, type the required learning coefficients and momentum coefficients.

4. Click **OK**.

Weight Updates

When using the steepest descent learning algorithm, the node input weights can be adjusted either after each pattern has been presented to the network or after an entire pass of patterns. Normally, the weights are updated after an entire pass.

To choose pattern or pass weight updates:

1. From the Multi-Layer Perceptron menu, choose **Dialog**.

2. In the Learning Rule group, click the **Wgt. update** drop-down list.

3. Click the desired weight updating strategy.

4. Click **OK**.

Node Input Weights

The Multi-Layer Perceptron begins training with random node input weights. However, as mentioned above, the choice of these weights can have a large effect on the performance of your network. Neural Connection, therefore, allows you to change the distribution pattern of the weight values and the range within which the values are chosen. It also allows you to change the seed for the random number generation.

The distribution functions allowed are uniform and Gaussian distributions.

Note: The Range option operates differently for uniform and Gaussian distributions. With a uniform distribution, the initial weights are randomly selected and have values that cannot exceed the range set. With a Gaussian distribution, the initial weights are randomly selected based on a Gaussian distribution with a variance equal to the selected range values.

To change the weight initialization values:

1. From the Multi-Layer Perceptron menu, choose **Dialog**.

2. In the Weights group, click the **Distribution** drop-down list.

3. Click the desired weight distribution.

4. In the **Range +/-** and **Seed** fields, type the distribution range and random seed number.

5. Click **OK**.

Normalization

Data normalization ensures that each input contributes equally to the decision or prediction made by the network.

If the input values were not normalized, an input that varied over the range 100 to 110 would be far more significant than one that varied over the range 1.0 to 2.0. In fact, the first input, although of greater absolute magnitude, varies by only 10%, while the second varies by 100%.

To normalize data at the input layer:

1. From the Multi-Layer Perceptron menu, choose **Dialog**.

2. In the Input Layer group, click the **Normalization** drop-down list.

3. Click **Standard.**

4. Click **OK**.

To normalize data at the output layer:

1. From the Multi-Layer Perceptron menu, choose **Dialog**.

2. In the Output Layer group, click the **Normalization** drop-down list.

3. Click **Standard.**

4. Click **OK**.

Saved Settings

As explained in Appendix I, a Neural Connection application is saved as a text file with an *.nni* extension. Within the file, each tool has its own text commands that set up the tool when it is loaded into Neural Connection. Some of these can be altered in text form, but it is strongly recommended that any changes be made using Neural Connection's workspace.

The application can be loaded into Neural Connection by using the **Open** command on the File menu.

An example of a saved Multi-Layer Perceptron is given below. Some of the text has been omitted, indicated by the elipses (…).

```
[Multi-Layer Perceptron]
.Name=MLP1
.GridX=17
.GridY=20
Version="1.0"
Function1="Tanh"
Function2="Tanh"
AutoHid=TRUE
Update="Epoch"
Algorithm="ConjGrad"
Distribution="Uniform"
LearnCoeff1=0.89999997615814208984
MaxRecs1=100
MaxUpdates1=100
MomentCoeff1=0.10000000149011611938
LearnCoeff2=0.69999998807907104492
MaxRecs2=500
MaxUpdates2=100
MomentCoeff2=0.40000000596046447754
LearnCoeff3=0.5
MaxRecs3=526
MaxUpdates3=100
MomentCoeff3=0.5
LearnCoeff4=0.40000000596046447754
MaxRecs4=526
MaxUpdates4=10000
MomentCoeff4=0.60000002384185791016
nHid1=6
nHid2=0
NormInputs="Standard"
NormOutputs="Standard"
Range=0.10000000149011611938
RandSeed=1
```

```
TrnStop=0.0010000000474974513054
ValStop=0.0010000000474974513054
TrnPCStop=95
ValPCStop=95
BestNetwork=TRUE
ObjectiveFunction="Unknown"
ProblemType=PREDICTION
NumTrainRecs=526
NumValidRecs=113
NumInputs=41
NumTargets=1
WeightsInit=TRUE
Built=TRUE
DataSet=VALIDATION
NumWeights=259
CurrWeights0=-0.07908985019,-1.014111519,-0.4921611249,
0.001227377797,-0.6124492288,-0.4818901122,-0.1240925193,
…
0.005752544384,0.5810804963,0.01546239201,0.03217257559,
0.2027864903,0.1256297529,-0.2631931305
BestWeights0=0.009626412764,-0.0594666861,0.07375947386,-
0.007460379507,-0.06034648418,-0.05716620386,0.09768972546,
…
0.03358019516,0.02640005387,-_0.0476292856,0.06332649291
BestTrainError=1.0061955451965332031
BestTrainCorrect=0
BestValidError=1.0068527460098266602
BestValidCorrect=0
UpdateDirection0=-6.589657307,-59.07694244,-5.022693634,
22.46180725,-20.38725281,-6.423611641,8.843470573,0.3815702796,
…
1.4892416,13.59504795,-20.87311935,22.35206604,-10.07636929,-
16.06119347
GradientMag=1161.3455810546875
NumUpdates=23
TotalUpdates=23
TrainStage=0
InputNorm=41,639,41,36.24412918,840.0062256,4.117371082,-
216.4319153,597.8654175,9.003129959,1.
…
0.4999993742,0.4104036987,0.1654555649
TargetNorm=1,639,1,0.4945336908,1,0.2499970004,1,0.4999699891
```

Radial Basis Function

Chapter 7.2

Overview

The Radial Basis Function is a modeling and forecasting tool that uses a neural network to model your data. It can be used to classify patterns or to predict values from your data. Because it uses a supervised learning technique, it requires your data to contain targets for training the network.

This chapter provides the following information:

- Explains why the Radial Basis Function is useful

- Gives an introduction to the ideas behind the Radial Basis Function

- Explains how to train the Radial Basis Function

- Explains how to improve the results produced by the Radial Basis Function

Why Use a Radial Basis Function?

Radial Basis Functions are good at modeling data, even when they contain nonlinearities. Their main advantage over the Multi-Layer Perceptron is that, since they train in one stage rather than using an iterative process, they can produce results in a shorter time.

If you are trying to solve a problem in which the input data are corrupted with additive noise, a Radial Basis Function is particularly useful. This is because it can be shown that the best-fitting function for the true data in such a situation is a linear combination of nonlinear basis functions, and thus, they can be directly modeled by a Radial Basis Function.

For a decision problem, it is useful for the outputs of your network to reflect the likelihood of a given data set belonging to a particular decision class. If the error of a Radial Basis Function is minimized correctly, it automatically produces outputs that sum to unity, and that, therefore, represent a probability for the outputs.

What Is a Radial Basis Function?

The Radial Basis Function object is a general-purpose neural network tool. It is a supervised, feed-forward neural network with one hidden layer of artificial neurons. It differs from Perceptron-based networks in two ways.

First, the outputs that form the hidden layer are not simply the product of the input data and a weighting. Instead, the inputs to each node, or artificial neuron, are treated as a measure of how far away the data are from a center. This center can be viewed as the position of the node in a spatial system that is defined by the input fields of the data. This is sometimes known as the *data space*.

Second, the transfer functions of the nodes are governed by nonlinear functions that can be said to be an approximation of the influence that data points have at the center. Transfer functions dictate the level of output from a node and replace the threshold, on or off mechanism of biological neurons, with an output that varies with the input. The transfer functions used are known as *radial basis* functions—hence, the name of this type of neural network.

This results in a linear combination of nonlinear basis functions and means that once a network has been trained, solutions can be found for any specific data input.

The most common transfer functions used in Radial Basis Functions are radial spline, Gaussian, and power functions.

In effect, a Radial Basis Function solves problems by looking at clusters of data rather than at boundaries between data.

Training

To train the Radial Basis Function:

*   From the Radial Basis Function menu, choose **Train**. Neural Connection displays the RBF Performance window during training.

The Radial Basis Function trains in one iteration, which makes training very rapid. However, to get the best results from a Radial Basis Function, the best number of centers must be chosen before training. Since it is not possible to know in advance the best number of centers, the Radial Basis Function trains with an increasing number of centers and, after training stops, uses the model with the lowest validation set error.

To stop training:

1. In the RBF Performance window, click **STOP**.

2. Click **Exit**.

If training is not stopped manually, the Radial Basis Function stops training

*   When it reaches the maximum number of centers

*   If the centers are being positioned by a sample strategy, when it has the same number of centers as there are records in the training data

*   If the Optimization facility is not enabled, after training the number of centers set in the Centers field

    or

    When instructed to stop by the **Stop When** facility.

The Stop When Facility

The Stop When facility is a procedure that enables a Radial Basis Function to select an optimum network architecture, within boundaries that you choose.

Initially, as the Radial Basis Function adds centers during training, it becomes increasingly good at predicting the correct results. Then a plateau is reached where adding centers to the network does not improve the response. This is followed by another increase in accuracy. Eventually, if it continues adding centers, your network predicts the training results perfectly.

However, feeding test data into this network gives results that are not very accurate. This is because the network learned the training data exactly, rather than producing a generalization. It was overtrained.

In fact, the optimum performance of the network is obtained at the plateau point, and the Stop When facility is designed to stop training when this plateau point is reached.

The Stop When facility uses a measurement of change in error to decide when the network has the optimum number of centers and training should stop. The Radial Basis Function looks back at the number of previous passes designated in the **Measured over x epochs** field and, if the error change over this period is greater than the threshold set in the **Change in Error** field, stops training.

Changing the Optimization Parameters

> *Note:* *These features can be used only if the Center Optimization option has been enabled.*

To change the size of the error change threshold:

1. From the Radial Basis Function menu, choose **Dialog**.

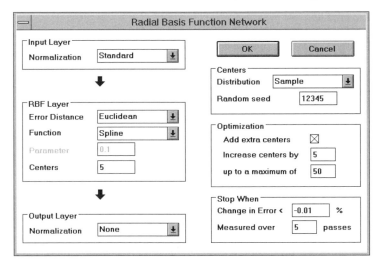

The Radial Basis Function dialog window

2. In the Stop When group's **Change in Error** field, type the value required.

3. Click **OK**.

To change the number of trials over which the gradient variance is measured:

1. From the Radial Basis Function menu, choose **Dialog**.

2. In the Stop When group's **Measured over x epochs** field, type the number of trials required.

3. Click **OK**.

When calculating the performance of each trial, the Radial Basis Function can use one of two error distance measuring techniques—Euclidean or City Block. A Euclidean measurement gives greater accuracy but can take longer to calculate.

To select the error distance measuring technique:

1. From the Radial Basis Function menu, choose **Dialog**.

2. In the RBF Layer group, click the **Error Distance** drop-down list.

3. Click the desired error distance measuring technique.

4. Click **OK**.

Improving Your Results

The decisions that affect the performance of your network include:

- The number of nodes, or centers

- The positioning of the centers

- The nonlinear function chosen as the transfer function

- The parameters of the nonlinear functions

- The weights for the inputs to the final network layer

- The use of confidence outputs

The Number of Centers

If you do not want to use the Optimization facility, the Radial Basis Function is trained once, with a fixed number of centers.

To choose a fixed number of centers:

1. From the Radial Basis Function menu, choose **Dialog**.

2. In the Optimization group, disable the Optimization facility by deselecting **Add extra centers**.

3. In the **Centers** field in the RBF Layer group, type the required number of centers.

4. Click **OK**.

If the Optimization facility is enabled, the Radial Basis Function trains between the number of centers set in the RBF Layer group and a maximum number of centers. The training takes place in trials which are an incremental number of centers apart.

To enable the Optimization facility:

1. From the Radial Basis Function menu, choose **Dialog**.

2. In the Optimization group, select **Add extra centers.**

3. Click **OK**.

To set the maximum number of centers:

1. From the Radial Basis Function menu, choose **Dialog**.

2. In the Optimization group's **up to a maximum of** field, type the required number of centers.

3. Click **OK**.

To select the trial increment:

1. From the Radial Basis Function menu, choose **Dialog**.

2. In the Optimization group's **Increase centers by** field, type the required increment.

3. Click **OK**.

Positioning the Centers

Where the centers are positioned also affects the performance of your network. Neural Connection allows you to choose between three different center positioning strategies.

Sample   The centers are placed on selected data points.

Random   The centers are distributed randomly throughout the data space.

Trial   The first center is placed by a sample strategy, and then others are placed on outlying data points only.

To choose the center strategy to be used:

1. From the Radial Basis Function menu, choose **Dialog**.

2. In the Centers groups's **Distribution** field, click the drop-down list.

3. Click the desired center placing strategy.

4. Click **OK**.

Choosing the Nonlinear Function

The choice of nonlinear function is not usually a major factor in network performance, unless there is an inherent special symmetry in the problem.

Neural Connection has four nonlinear functions—Spline, Gaussian, Multi-Quadratic, and Inverse Multi-Quadratic.

The Spline and Multi-Quadratic functions increase with distance from the center, while the Gaussian and Inverse Multi-Quadratic functions decrease.

Spline $\mathbf{d}^2\log\mathbf{d}$

Gaussian e^{-d2/β^2}

Multi-Quadratic $(\mathbf{d}^2+\beta^2)$

Inverse Multi-Quadratic $1/(\mathbf{d}^2+\beta^2)$

where $\mathbf{d}$ is the distance from the center and ß is a parameter.

To choose the nonlinear function:

1. From the Radial Basis Function menu, choose **Dialog**.

2. In the RBF Layer group's **Function** field, click the drop-down list.

3. Click the desired nonlinear function.

4. Click **OK**.

The Nonlinear Function Parameters

Choosing the smoothing parameter for the nonlinear function is sometimes more important than the choice of actual function. The parameters of the Gaussian, Multi Quadratic, and Inverse Multi-Quadratic functions can be changed in the Radial Basis Function.

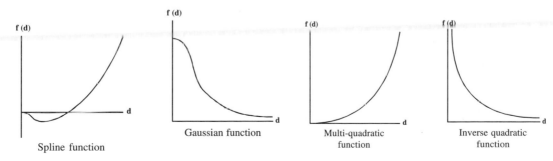

Spline function   Gaussian function   Multi-quadratic function   Inverse quadratic function

To change the nonlinear function parameter:

1. From the Radial Basis Function menu, choose **Dialog**.

2. In the RBF Layer group's **Parameter** field, type the desired value.

3. Click **OK**.

Note: *The default parameter for the Gaussian nonlinear function may be too low for many applications. Better results may be achieved by setting the parameter to 0.5 or greater.*

Final Layer Weights

It is possible to show that the problem of deciding the weighting of inputs from the hidden layer to the final layer of the network can be reduced to a solvable least squares problem. Thus, knowing both the network outputs and the target outputs, Neural Connection can minimize the error by automatically adjusting the weightings.

Confidence Outputs

Confidence outputs are a second set of outputs that can be generated by the Radial Basis Function. When a model is built, a second radial basis function learns the relationship between the inputs and the level of error being generated by the network. This enables it to predict error levels when the network is run.

When you select Confidence Outputs, the Radial Basis Function generates two outputs—the actual output of the Radial Basis Function (where it predicts the target field) and the confidence output. The confidence output is in the same units as the target field and can be viewed as a likely maximum error for that particular output.

To generate confidence outputs:

1. From the Radial Basis Function menu, choose **Dialog**.

2. In the Output Layer group, select **Confidence Outputs**.

3. Click **OK**.

Normalization

Data normalization ensures that each input contributes equally to the decision or prediction made by the network.

If the input values were not normalized, an input that varied over the range 100 to 110 would be far more significant than one that varied over the range 1.0 to 2.0. In fact, the first input, although of greater absolute magnitude, varies by only 10%, while the second varies by 100%.

To normalize data at the input layer:

1. From the Radial Basis Function menu, choose **Dialog**.

2. In the Input Layer group, click the **Normalization** drop-down list.

3. Click **Standard.**

4. Click **OK**.

To normalize data at the output layer:

1. From the Radial Basis Function menu, choose **Dialog**.

2. In the Output Layer group, click the **Normalization** drop-down list.

3. Click **Standard.**

4. Click **OK**.

Saved Settings

As explained in Appendix I, a Neural Connection application is saved as a text file with an *.nni* extension. Within the file, each tool has its own text commands that set up the tool when it is loaded into Neural Connection. Some of these can be altered in text form, but it is strongly recommended that any changes be made using Neural Connection's workspace.

The application can be loaded into Neural Connection by using the **Open** command on the File menu.

An example of a saved Radial Basis Function is given below. Some of the text has been omitted, indicated by the elipses (...).

```
[Radial Basis Function]
.Name=RBF5
.GridX-14
.GridY=12
Version="1.0"
Distribution="Sample"
Function="Spline"
Parameter=0.10000000000000000555
NormInputs="Standard"
```

```
NormTargets="Standard"
StopEpochs=5
StopError=-0.009999999776
Centres=40
MaxCentres=50
IncreaseCentres=1
RandSeed=12345
ErrorMeasure="Euclidean"
AddCentres=FALSE
SolverMethod="QRD"
DirectInput=FALSE
EnableConfidence=FALSE
ObjectiveFunction="Unknown"
CentreMatrix=40
Centre1=8,1.675935745,-0.04677049443,-0.8019070625,
2.27803421,1.58421731,-0.390635699,-0.638348639,-1.165304065
Centre2=8,1.520033717,0.3517134786,0.2058656514,0.7764872909,
0.1436098516,-0.390635699,-0.638348639,0.8581451774
…
Centre40=8,0.8982813954,1.148681402,-0.5490735769,1.371302962,-
1.008876204,-0.390635699,-0.638348639,0.8581451774
InputNorm=8,639,8,840.0062256,4.117371082,-216.4319153,
597.8654175,9.003129959,1.547730803,0.2895148695,0.5758998394,
8,290305.1563,6.297646523,709725.25,171043.0625,48.18464661,
1.966031551,0.2056960166,0.2442392111,8,538.7997437,2.509511232,
842.45190_43,413.5735168,6.941515923,1.402152419,0.4535372257,
0.4942056239
TargetNorm=1,639,1,0.4945226908,1,0.249970004,1,0.4999699891
MinValErr=101.8553314
MinTrnErr=470.4565735
NumTrainRecs=526
NumValidRecs=113
NumInputs=8
NumTargets=1
ProblemType=PREDICTION
LargestCentres=40
Built=TRUE
Trained=TRUE
CentreMin=40
CentreMax=40
BufferedTRecs=0
BufferedVRecs=0
Qrd=40,1,1,41
QrdVector1=42,789254.89959323813673,0.50805599908129361886,
0.48370863270275310519,0.32768743756201412776,
0.50862160503339493012,0.39701774459446442789,
…
QrdVector40=3,20.273823615223342642,-0.01436365380194115117,-
0.1262827020407392975
QrdVector41=2,0.15140072419722053199,-2.9540843886353100878
NumberUpdates=0
BestValCorrect=100
BestTrnCorrect=100
```

Bayesian Network Tool

Chapter 7.3

Overview

The Bayesian Network is a modeling and forecasting tool that uses a neural network to model your data. It can be used to classify patterns or to predict values from your data. Because it uses a supervised learning technique, it requires that your data contain targets for training the network.

This chapter provides the following information:

- Explains why the Bayesian Network is useful

- Gives an introduction to the ideas behind the Bayesian Network

- Explains how to train the Bayesian Network

- Explains how to improve the results produced by the Bayesian Network

Why Use a Bayesian Network?

Bayesian Networks are similar in structure to Multi-Layer Perceptrons but with several important modifications. They also have a number of advantages over the Radial Basis Function and the Multi-Layer Perceptron. The most significant advantage is that the algorithm used does not require a validation data set in order to produce a generalized model. With Radial Basis Functions and Multi-Layer Perceptrons, the validation set is essential to prevent overtraining. The Bayesian Network algorithm automatically prevents this. As a result, the Bayesian Network requires less data and is thus particularly useful when you have a limited data set or when your data are very sparse.

What Is a Bayesian Network?

The principals behind Bayesian statistics were produced over 200 years ago. However, despite being well-understood, it wasn't until the 1930's that the theories were put to a practical use.

Bayesian statistics concentrate on how probabilities are affected by prior and posterior knowledge—by what we know about a situation before and after we examine the data. Bayes' rule states that the probability of the network being in a state w, given that an event D has occured, is equal to the likelihood that the event D would occur if the network was in state w, multiplied by the probability of the network being in the state w regardless of any events, divided by the probability of the event D occuring, regardless of the state of the network.

This is sometimes shown as:

$$\text{Posterior} = \frac{(\text{Likelihood x Prior})}{\text{Evidence}}$$

Rather than using a new neural network architecture, Bayesian statistics allow us to apply this probabilistic approach to an existing type of network.

The Bayesian Network is the application of Bayesian statistics to the Multi-Layer Perceptron and as such has many features in common with that neural network. The major difference is in the way that the error measure, or accuracy of the network, is calculated.

In conventional Multi-Layer Perceptrons, the learning rule changes the weights on connections to minimize an error measure. This error measure is usually a sum-of-squares error measure. Because training sets are finite, there is a risk that the networks will learn the noise in the problem as well as the underlying function. Bayesian theory adds an extra term to the error measure in order to reduce the impact of noise on the network. This enables the network to generalize without needing to use a validation data set.

The extra term enables you to select parameter groups to use to evaluate this term. The parameter groups that you select have a big impact on the results achieved.

Training

To train the Bayesian Network:

- From the Bayesian Network menu, choose **Train**. Neural Connection displays the Bayesian Performance window during training.

Stopping Training

Training can be stopped at any time by clicking **STOP** in the Training Dialog box. This may be necessary when the Bayesian Network takes a long time to find a global minimum error that satisfies the stopping criteria.

To stop training:

1. In the Bayesian Performance window, click **STOP**.

2. Click **Exit**.

If training is not stopped manually, the Bayesian Network stops training:

- When it reaches the maximum number of epochs

- When instructed to stop by the Stopping Conditions facility

The Stopping Conditions Facility

This procedure enables a Bayesian Network to select an optimum network architecture, within boundaries that you choose.

Initially, as the Bayesian Network trains, it becomes increasingly good at predicting the correct results. Then a plateau is reached, where further training iterations do not improve the response. The optimum performance of the network is obtained at the plateau point and the Stopping Conditions facility is designed to stop training when this plateau point is reached.

The Stopping Conditions facility uses a measurement of change in error to decide when the network has the optimum point and training should stop. The Bayesian Network looks back at the number of previous passes designated in the **Window size** field and, if the error change over this period is less than the threshold set in the **Gradient** field, stops training.

Improving Your Results

The decisions that affect the performance of your Bayesian Network are:

- Whether to use validation data for training

- The number of hidden layers

- The number of nodes in a layer

- The choice of parameter groups

- The initial parameter weights

- Output layer options

Normalization

Data normalization ensures that each input contributes equally to the decision or prediction made by the network.

If the input values were not normalized, an input that varied over the range 100 to 110 would be far more significant than one that varied over the range 1.0 to 2.0. In fact, the first input, although of greater absolute magnitude, varies by only 10%, while the second varies by 100%.

Unlike the Multi-Layer Perceptron and Radial Basis Function, the Bayesian Network automatically normalizes data.

Using Validation Data

When you use the Bayesian Network, you can choose to use validation data for training. When this happens, the validation data set is incorporated into the training data set. This increases the amount of data that is available during training. However, the Committee Decision option of Multiple Networks requires a validation set to be present, so if you intend to use this option, you should not use the validation data set for training.

To use the validation data set for training:

1. From the Bayesian Network menu, choose **Dialog**.

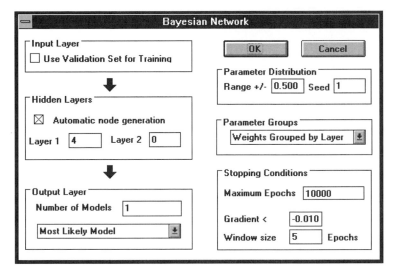

Bayesian Network dialog box

2. In the Input Layer group, select **Use Validation Set for Training**.

The Number of Hidden Layers

In Neural Connection, Bayesian Networks can have either one or two hidden layers. This can either be decided automatically, based on the data presented to the Bayesian Network, or it can be set manually.

In most problems, a second hidden layer does not produce a large improvement in performance.

To choose the number of hidden layers:

1. From the Bayesian Network menu, choose **Dialog**.

2. In the Hidden Layers group, deselect **Automatic node generation**.

3. In the **Layer** fields, type the number of nodes that you want to use. To not use a layer, type 0 in its field.

4. Click **OK**.

The Number of Nodes in Each Layer

The number of nodes in a layer can either be selected automatically by Neural Connection or it can be set independently. In most cases, increasing the number of nodes improves the performance of the Bayesian Network on the training data but not necessarily on test data.

If you add enough hidden units, the network will achieve 100% correct results on its training set because it will have enough weights to represent exactly all of the training patterns. This would, however, be an extremely poor network because it would have little ability to generalize or find solutions for examples that it had not been trained on.

The correct way to assess the impact of the number of hidden units on a problem is to look at performance on a test set. As the total number of hidden units increases from one, the network performance on the test data increases rapidly. This is because each new hidden unit starts to represent one of the underlying features in the data set.

As more units are added, performance levels off. Adding further units may then cause a decrease in performance because the power of generalization is lost and the network begins to learn the noise present in the data.

It is best to use as few nodes as possible to achieve the desired result.

To set the number of nodes in a layer:

1. From the Bayesian Network menu, choose **Dialog**.

2. In the Hidden Layers group, deselect **Automatic node generation**.

3. In the **Layer** field of the appropriate layer, type the desired number of nodes.

4. Click **OK**.

Parameter Groups

In a conventional Multi-Layer Perceptron, the weights between neurons are adapted during training. In a Bayesian Network, both these weights and a set of parameters can be altered. These parameters can be set up in a variety of ways. The higher the number of parameter groups that are used, the greater the degree of freedom available to the network.

There are four options:

Single Weight Group   No parameter learning takes place.

Weights Grouped by Layer   One parameter group is created for each layer of connections. For a single hidden layer of neurons, there are two parameter groups. For two hidden layers, there are three parameter groups.

Separate Weights and Biases The weights and the bias weights are treated separately. For a single hidden layer of neurons, there are four parameter groups. For two hidden layers, there are six parameter groups.

Automatic Relevance Detection Rather than basing the parameter groups around layers of weights, they are based around weights from an input. The number of groups becomes dependent on the number of neurons in the input layer. This approach allows the network to determine the relative influence of the inputs and to penalize those inputs that are noisy.

Parameter Values

The Bayesian Network begins training with random parameter values. However, the choice of these values can have a large effect on the performance of your network. Neural Connection, therefore, allows you to change the range within which the values are chosen and the seed for the random number generation.

To change the parameter initialization values:

1. From the Bayesian Network menu, choose **Dialog**.

2. In the **Range +/-** and **Seed** fields, type the distribution range and random seed number.

3. Click **OK**.

Output Layer Options

Multiple Models

It is possible to configure the Bayesian Network to train and use multiple models.

When you select a number of models greater than one, several different models are generated during the training process. Each is initialized with a different set of starting weights but uses the same data set to train on.

After you have trained multiple models, when running your data you can choose to use either the **Most Likely Model** or the **Committee Decision** option.

Most Likely Model

This option examines the cost functions for each of the models that have been built and selects the model with the best cost function over the training set. This model is then used when the model is run.

Committee Decision

This option uses the error on the validation data set to give a relative likelihood for each model. When data is run through the Bayesian Network, all the models created during training are used, with the final result generated for a record being a combination of the results from the different models, depending on the relative likelihood of the individual model.

This has the effect of reinforcing accurate training but of weakening inaccurate training. As a result, it can indicate very well when you have failed to build a successful model but it should not be used for propensity type applications.

Note: Committee Decision can be used only when the Validation data set is not used as part of the training set.

Saved Settings

As explained in Appendix I, a Neural Connection application is saved as a text file with an *.nni* extension. Within the file, each tool has its own text commands that set up the tool when it is loaded into Neural Connection. Some of these can be altered in text form, but it is strongly recommended that any changes be made using Neural Connection's workspace.

The application can be loaded into Neural Connection by using the **Open** command on the File menu.

An example of a saved Bayesian Network is shown below:

```
[Bayesian Network]
.Name=Bayes1
.GridX=14
.GridY=13
Version="1.0"
Function1="Sigmoid"
Function2="Linear"
AutoHid=TRUE
Update="Epoch"
Algorithm="ConjGrad"
Distribution="Gaussian"
nHid1=1
nHid2=0
NormInputs="Standard"
NormOutputs="Standard"
Range=0.5
RandSeed=1
ObjectiveFunction="Unknown"
ProblemType=PREDICTION
NumTrainRecs=0
NumValidRecs=0
NumInputs=0
NumTargets=0
WeightsInit=FALSE
Built=FALSE
TrainOnValidation=FALSE
DataSet=TRAIN
NumWeights=0
NumModels=1
NumGroups=0
GroupStyle="OnePerLayer"
OutputStyle="WinnerTakeAll"
Model0=9.051306501e-037
CostFunction=8.018149939e-039,8.018149939e-039,8.018149939e-
039,8.018149939e-039,8.018149939e-039,8.018149939e-039,8.018149939e-
039,8.018149939e-039,8.018149939e-039
WeightGroupX0=8.018149939e-039,8.018149939e-039,8.018149939e-
039,8.018149939e-039,8.018149939e-039,8.018149939e-039,8.018149939e-
039,8.018149939e-039,8.018149939e-039,8.018149939e-039,8.018149939e-
039,8.018149939e-039,8.018149939e-039,8.018149939e-0
_39,8.018149939e-039,8.018149939e-039,8.018149939e-039,8.018149939e-
039,8.018149939e-039,8.018149939e-039,8.018149939e-039,8.018149939e-
039,8.018149939e-039,8.018149939e-039,8.018149939e-039,8.018149939e-
039,8.018149939e-039,8.018149939e-039,8.018149
_939e-039,8.018149939e-039,8.018149939e-039,8.018149939e-
```

039,8.018149939e-
039,8.018149939e-039,8.018149939e-039,8.018149939e-039,8.018149939e-
039,8.018149939e-039,8.018149939e-039,8.018149939e-039,8.018149939e-
039,8.018149939e-039,8.018149939e-039,8.
_018149939e-039,8.018149939e-039,8.018149939e-039,8.018149939e-
039,8.018149939e-039,8.018149939e-039,8.018149939e-039,8.018149939e-
039,8.018149939e-039,8.018149939e-039,8.018149939e-039,8.018149939e-
039,8.018149939e-039,8.018149939e-039,8.018149939e-
_039,8.018149939e-039,8.018149939e-039,8.018149939e-039,8.018149939e-
039,8.018149939e-039,8.018149939e-039,8.018149939e-039,8.018149939e-
039,8.018149939e-039,8.018149939e-039,8.018149939e-039,8.018149939e-
039,8.018149939e-039,8.018149939e-039,8.01814
_9939e-039,8.018149939e-039,8.018149939e-039,8.018149939e-
039,8.018149939e-039,8.018149939e-039,8.018149939e-039,8.018149939e-
039,8.018149939e-039,8.018149939e-039,8.018149939e-039,8.018149939e-
039,8.018149939e-039,8.018149939e-039,8.018149939e-039,8
_.018149939e-039,8.018149939e-039,8.018149939e-039,8.018149939e-
039,8.018149939e-039,8.018149939e-039,8.018149939e-039,8.018149939e-
039,8.018149939e-039,8.018149939e-039,8.018149939e-039,8.018149939e-
039,8.018149939e-039
Scales=8.018149939e-039,8.018149939e-039,8.018149939e-
039,8.018149939e-
039,8.018149939e-039,8.018149939e-039,8.018149939e-039,8.018149939e-
039,8.018149939e-039,8.018149939e-039
GradientMag=1
NumUpdates=0
TotalUpdates=20311
TrainStage=0
BestModel=0

Kohonen Network Tool

Chapter 7.4

Overview

The Kohonen network tool is an unsupervised neural network technique. It builds its own representations of the data and can be used as a clustering or segmentation tool or to remove nondiscriminatory information from the data set.

This chapter provides the following information:

- Explains why the Kohonen tool is useful

- Gives an overview of how the Kohonen tool works

- Explains how to train the Kohonen tool

- Explains how to tailor the results from the Kohonen tool

Why Use the Kohonen Tool?

The Kohonen tool enables you to reduce the dimensionality of data sets by representing multi-input data as a one- or two-dimensional array of artificial neurons. It can thus be used to preprocess your data before they are fed into another modeling tool.

It can also be used to examine clusters in your data and to assign new examples to a particular cluster.

What Is a Kohonen Network?

The Kohonen self-organizing map was invented by Professor Teuvo Kohonen and is closely modeled on the way that certain parts of the brain are known to work.

Some parts of the brain perform specific tasks, such as sensing touch or hearing, and it has been found that the neurons in these areas are spatially ordered so that, for example, one group of neurons responds to high frequency sounds and another to low frequency sounds.

Kohonen networks make the basic assumption that clusters, or classes, are formed from patterns that share common features and group similar patterns together. To do this, Kohonen networks are usually one- or two-dimensional grids of artificial neurons, or nodes, where every node in the grid is connected to all the inputs. There is no separate output layer, as the output comes directly from the grid of neurons (known as the *Kohonen layer*).

Each artificial neuron is linked to each of the inputs with a weight and can be thought of as being at a point in the input data-space. Before training starts, these weights are set to initial values.

When a pattern is presented to the grid, the artificial neuron that is most like the input pattern is found. This artificial neuron then has its weights altered to make it more like the input pattern. To enable the Kohonen layer to group similar patterns, a neighborhood of artificial neurons around the winning artificial neuron is also altered to be more like the input pattern. This is equivalent to moving the node towards the position of the example in the input data-space.

The result of this process is that, after a number of passes of the data set through the Kohonen layer, different areas of the Kohonen layer respond to different types of examples within the data set.

Training

To train the Kohonen tool:

- From the Kohonen tool menu, choose **Train**. Neural Connection displays the Kohonen Performance window during training.

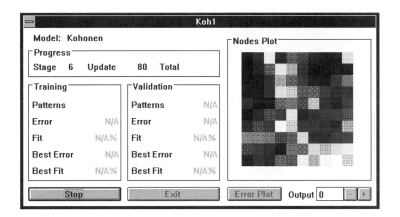

The Training Performance window

The Kohonen Performance window displays the stage that training has reached and a nodes plot. The nodes plot is a representation of how tightly clustered the artificial neurons are in the input data-space. Nodes that are tightly grouped in the input data-space imply that there is a lot of activity in that part of the data-space and that a cluster of examples is present.

The nodes plot represents each artificial neuron in a one- or two-dimensional layer as a square, which is colored according to how close it is to its neighboring neurons. If it is close to its neighbors, it is shown as a light color; if it is distant from its neighbors, it is shown as a dark color.

Note: The colors shown for a neuron in the node plot correspond to its closeness to its neighbors, relative to the closeness of the other nodes to their neighbors. There is always a neuron that is closer to its neighbors than other neurons. This may result in instability between training runs.

Stopping Training

To stop training:

1. In the Performance window, click **STOP**.

2. Click **Exit**.

The Kohonen tool stops training when every example in the data has been passed through the Kohonen layer a certain number of times.

To change the number of passes:

1. From the Kohonen tool menu, choose **Dialog**.

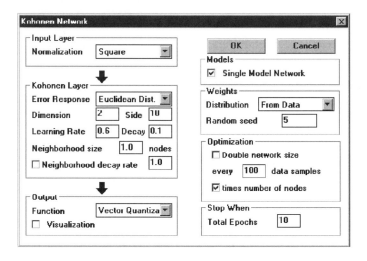

Kohonen dialog box

2. In the Stop When group's **Total Epochs** field, type the required number of passes through the data.

3. Click **OK**.

Tailoring Your Result

Four major aspects of the Kohonen tool can be tailored to fit your problem:

*   Kohonen layer initialization conditions

*   The Kohonen layer topology

*   Training conditions

*   The output function

Initialization Conditions

The initial weights in the Kohonen layer can be distributed in five ways. The random number seed used in distributing the weights can be set so that experiments can be reproduced.

Small Random The weights are set to small random values between -0.1 and 0.1.

Random The weights are set to random values between -1 and 1.

From Data The weights are set by taking random samples from within the input data set.

Small Grid The initial weights are distributed in a small grid pattern.

Grid The initial weights are distributed in a grid pattern.

To choose the Kohonen layer weight distribution method:

1. From the Kohonen tool menu, choose **Dialog**.

2. In the Weights group's **Distribution** field, click the drop-down list.

3. Click the desired weight distribution method.

4. Click **OK**.

To set the random number seed:

1. From the Kohonen tool menu, choose **Dialog**.

2. In the Weights group's **Random seed** field, type the desired random number seed.

3. Click **OK**.

Kohonen Layer Topology

The topology of the Kohonen Layer is fixed using these controls.

Dimensionality

The Kohonen layer can have a one or two dimensional topology.

To set the dimensionality:

1. From the Kohonen tool menu, choose **Dialog**.

2. In the Kohonen Layer group's **Dimension** field, type the desired dimension.

3. Click **OK**.

Sidelength

The sidelength of the Kohonen layer can be set. However, if node construction is taking place through optimization, the set sidelength may change during training.

By setting the sidelength, you specify the number of artificial neurons, or nodes, that the Kohonen layer contains. The number of nodes is simply the sidelength raised to the power of the dimensionality of the Kohonen layer.

Note: A sidelength cannot result in a topology with more nodes than there are data examples in the training set. The number of examples gives the upper limit of nodes unless Node Construction is being used. When multiple models are being trained, each model is given a number of nodes that is not greater than the number of examples in that class.

To set the sidelength:

1. From the Kohonen tool menu, choose **Dialog**.

2. In the Kohonen Layer group's **Side** field, type the desired sidelength.

3. Click **OK**.

Training Conditions

Neighborhood Size

The neighborhood refers to the area around a winning node that is modified along with that node. The neighborhood size can be fixed or it can be allowed to decay by a percentage per training iteration. The advantage of decreasing the neighborhood size is that, as training proceeds, areas of the Kohonen layer become more sharply defined with regard to specific example types.

*Note: Even if the neighborhood size is fixed, if **Double network** size has been enabled, neighborhood size will decay as a proportion of the total number of nodes.*

The neighborhood size can be set to an initial value.

To set the neighborhood size:

1. From the Kohonen tool menu, choose **Dialog**.

2. In the Kohonen Layer group's **Neighborhood size** field, type the desired size.

3. Click **OK**.

To switch neighborhood size decay on or off:

1. From the Kohonen tool menu, choose **Dialog**.

2. In the Kohonen Layer group, select **Neighborhood decay rate**.

3. Click **OK**.

To change the neighborhood size decay rate:

1. From the Kohonen tool menu, choose **Dialog**.

2. In the Kohonen Layer group's **Neighborhood decay rate** field, type the desired decay rate.

3. Click **OK**.

Number of Models

When you are solving a problem with a symbolic output, the Kohonen module can be set to run one or multiple Kohonen layer modules. Running one model maps all the features of the input data to a single Kohonen layer. Running more than one model creates a number of Kohonen layers equal to the number of classes in the problem. Each Kohonen layer model is trained on data from one of the classes only. When an unknown piece of input data is presented when the object is run, the module assigns it to the class represented by the model that contains the winning node.

Creating more than one Kohonen layer is primarily useful for classification problems. Kohonen nets are not primarily classifiers in that they take data and organize them without knowing the classes to which they belong. Only after the layer has been trained are classes associated with areas of the topology. When data are intermingled, this may lead to some difficulty in assigning a node to a particular class. To avoid this problem, the Kohonen module can use the multi-model approach, looking at each class separately.

To switch multiple models on or off:

1. From the Kohonen tool menu, choose **Dialog**.

2. In the Models group, select or deselect **Single Model Network**.

3. Click **OK**.

Optimization: Node Construction

Node construction allows the fine tuning of the Kohonen layer by adding new nodes during the training process. When nodes are added to a Kohonen model, a new node is placed between every existing node. You cannot add nodes to a single node. There are two methods for adding nodes—Double Network Size and Times Number of Nodes.

Double Network Size   The Double Network Size method adds new nodes each time a set number of examples has been passed through the Kohonen layer.

Times Number of Nodes The Times Number of Nodes method adds new nodes each time that the product of a set number of data samples multiplied by the number of nodes have been passed through the Kohonen layer. This has the advantage of taking account of the longer time required for a large number of nodes to converge to a stable solution.

To switch on node construction:

1. From the Kohonen tool menu, choose **Dialog**.

2. In the Optimization group, select **Double network size**.

3. Click **OK**.

To change the frequency of node construction:

1. From the Kohonen tool menu, choose **Dialog**.

2. In the Optimization group's **every x data samples** field, type the desired number of data examples between periods of node construction.

3. Click **OK**.

To switch on the Times Number of Nodes option:

1. From the Kohonen tool menu, choose **Dialog**.

2. In the Optimization group, select **times number of nodes**.

3. Click **OK**.

Learning Rate

The learning rate sets the factors governing the change in the network weights. Both the initial learning rate and the decay of the learning rate can be fixed. The decay is fixed at a percentage per training pattern.

To change the learning rate:

1. From the Kohonen tool menu, choose **Dialog**.

2. In the Kohonen Layer group's **Learning Rate** field, type the desired learning rate.

3. Click **OK**.

To change the learning rate decay:

1. From the Kohonen tool menu, choose **Dialog**.

2. In the Kohonen Layer group's **Decay** field, type the desired learning rate decay.

3. Click **OK**.

Normalization

Two types of data normalization are possible—square and spherical.

Square Normalization   Square normalization normalizes input patterns to zero mean and unit variance over the training and validation data sets. It is recommended when using Euclidean distance response function with a minimum winner selection method.

Spherical Normalization   Spherical normalization normalizes each pattern to unit length, making the network lie on a unit sphere in the input space. It is recommended when using a dot product distance response function (see below) with a maximum winner selection method and can be selected only when a dot product response function has been selected.

To select a normalization procedure:

1. From the Kohonen tool menu, choose **Dialog**.

2. In the Input Layer group, click the **Normalization** drop-down list.

3. Click the desired normalization method.

4. Click **OK**.

Error Response Functions

The response function is the measure by which the winning node is chosen when input data are shown to the layer.

Euclidean Response Function   This function measures the Euclidean distance between the input data vector and the node weight vector. When it is selected, a minimum distance winner strategy is used; that is, the node with the closest weight vector to the input vector wins.

Dot Product Response Function   This function takes the dot product of the input data vector and the node weight vector. When it is selected, a maximum value winner strategy is used; that is, the node that produces the largest vector when dotted with the input data wins.

To choose an error response function:

1. From the Kohonen tool menu, choose **Dialog**.

2. In the Kohonen Layer group, click the **Error Response** drop-down list.

3. Click the desired error response function.

4. Click **OK**.

Output Function

The output function sets the output type from the nodes of the Kohonen Layer. Options include:

Vector Quantization   This sets the output of the Kohonen layer to the input space vector stored at the winning node.

VQ Codebook   This sets the output as a reference number to the winning node. It can be used only when one model is being trained.

Full Response   This causes output from every node in the network when shown an input pattern. For example, a network with 64 nodes (dimensionality 2, sidelength 8) will give an output with 64 fields.

To choose an output function:

1. From the Kohonen tool menu, choose **Dialog**.

2. In the Output group, click the **Function** drop-down list.

3. Click the desired output function.

4. Click **OK**.

Post Processing

Visualization provides a visual analysis of the network produced by the Kohonen module. When the topology is run, the final visual output of the network appears, along with the position in the input space of each node in the network.

When visualization has been selected, the Kohonen Network Viewer appears when the application is run. The Kohonen Network Viewer displays the final node plot of the training run.

The input space position of nodes are displayed on the left of the nodes plot. The input space coordinates of a specific node can be moved to the top of the list by using the mouse to click the node of interest.

	Meat	Frozen	Wines	Bakery
Node 1	0.00836	0.008776	0.000841	0.002047
Node 2	0.015714	0.031402	0.35247	0.005065
Node 3	0.123822	0.07887	0.02511	0.017816
Node 4	0.126069	0.109805	0.012975	0.00408
Node 5	0.42708	0.406463	0.009841	0.011109
Node 6	0.042614	0.049339	0.333433	0.028117
Node 7	0.26	0.038136	0.003299	0.001836

The Kohonen Network Viewer

Note: *If the node of interest is one of the last seven nodes, which can be found in the top right of the node plot, they may not be moved to the top of the node coordinates list because the list cannot scroll beyond the last node.*

Saved Settings

As explained in Appendix I, a Neural Connection application is saved as a text file with an *.nni* extension. Within the file, each tool has its own text commands that set up the tool when it is loaded into Neural Connection. Some of these can be altered in text form, but it is strongly recommended that any changes be made using Neural Connection's workspace.

The application can be loaded into Neural Connection by using the **Open** command on the File menu.

An example of a saved Kohonen Network is given below. Some of the text has been omitted, indicated by the elipses (…).

```
[Kohonen]
.Name=Koh1
.GridX=14
.GridY=19
Version="1.0"
SingleModel=TRUE
OutputFunction="VectQuant"
TopologyDimension=2
Side=10
LearningRate=0.6000000238
LearningDecay=0.1000000015
NeighbourhoodSizeFixed=FALSE
NbhoodSize=1
InitialNeighbourhoodProportion=0.1000000015
NbhoodDecay=1
StopEpochs=10
DoubleSize=FALSE
DoubleEvery=100
TimesNumNodes=TRUE
FieldNormFnType=1
FieldWidthType=1
Response="Euclidean"
NormInputs="Square"
WeightDist="Data"
RandSeed=5
Visualisation=FALSE
Threshold=3
UseThreshold=TRUE
NumModels=1
NumInputs=9
NumTargets=0
FirstPass=TRUE
InputNorm=9,227,9,0.7264472842,0.6418886185,0.4345261455,
0.7508051395,0.7500360012,0.7492668033,0.7484976649,
```

```
0.747728467,6.880314827,9,0.06885299832,0.08619196713,
0.06331780553,0.05917281657,0.05957692862,0.05997994542,
0.06038162857,0.06078227982,0.3_233314753,9,0.262398541,
0.2935846746,0.2516303062,0.2432546318,0.2440838516,
0.2449080348,0.2457267344,0.2465406209,0.5686224103
Trained=TRUE
Built=TRUE
VisTrained=FALSE
Mean=0
StandDev=0
ModelIteration1=288
ModelSetSize1=202
ModelTopology1=2,100,10
ModelDimension1=2
ModelSideLen1=10
ModelSizeFixed1=FALSE
ModelINSize1=1
ModelNSize1=0.05532684177
ModelINProp1=0.1000000015
ModelNProp1=0.00553268427
ModelNPropDecay1=1
ModelNumFields1=100
ModelFields1_1=9,9,-2.300487041,-2.048995972,-1.67202282,
-1.440486908,-1.432442069,-1.424480796,-1.416604757,
-1.408808231,-1.041534305,0,4.559930801,0,2,9,1,0
ModelFields1_2=9,9,-0.3253513873,-0.06548658758,0.09510280937,-
0.06793662906,-0.06455472112,-0.06119674444,-0.05786281079,-
0.0545518212,0.2418333888,0,0.8285109401,0,2,9,1,0
…
ModelFields1_100=9,9,0.2866048217,0.8380998969,1.211065054
-0.005313158501,0.002092498122,0.001157142571,0.004484576173,
0.007987003773,0.489043504,0,2.144625902,0,2,9,1,0
ModelVisVector1=1,0.838619411
ModelNumClasses1=0
ModelNormType1=1
ModelWidthType1=1
ModelRespType1=2
ModelInit1=0
ModelInitLrn1=0.6000000238
ModelLrnRate1=0.4497925341
ModelLrnDecay1=0.1000000015
ModelConstruction1=FALSE
ModelInitCPeriod1=100
ModelTimesNodes1=TRUE
ModelConstPeriod1=10000
```

Closest Class Mean Classifier

Chapter 7.5

Overview

The Closest Class Mean Classifier is a classification tool that uses statistical analysis to model your data.

Note: The Closest Class Mean classifier can be used for decision problems only.

This chapter provides the following information:

- Explains the ideas behind Closest Class Mean classification
- Explains how to use the Closest Class Mean tool

Note: The Closest Class Mean Classifier does not have a dialog box.

What Is Closest Class Mean Classification?

The Closest Class Mean (CCM) algorithm is a simple classifier that is easy to compute and that gives good results if the data examples for a decision class are well-clustered.

During the training phase, the CCM classifier computes a vector mean for each of the decision classes. The vector mean is a mean value calculated from the training data for each of the data attributes. In effect, the CCM classifier produces a typical example of each of the decision classes.

When you run the CCM classifier, the Euclidean distances between the new, unknown data vector and each of the class mean vectors are measured. The new vector is assigned to the class to which it is closest.

Although a CCM classifier is fast, it gives poor results if the training data contain a significant number of examples that are outside the clustered data. These tend to bias the class means and this leads to a poorer classification performance.

Using the Closest Class Mean Tool

To train the Closest Class Mean tool:

• From the Closest Class Mean menu, choose **Train**.

To view the mean class values:

• From the Closest Class Mean menu, choose **Print**.

Saved Settings

As explained in Appendix I, a Neural Connection application is saved as a text file with an *.nni* extension. Within the file, each tool has its own text commands that set up the tool when it is loaded into Neural Connection. Some of these can be altered in text form, but it is strongly recommended that any changes be made using Neural Connection's workspace.

The application can be loaded into Neural Connection by using the **Open** command on the File menu.

An example of a saved Closest Class Mean tool is shown below:

```
[Closest Class Mean]
.Name=Class1
.GridX=11
.GridY=13
ObjectiveFunction="Unknown"
Version="1.0"
NumInputs=4
NumClasses=3
NumMembers=40,40,40
ClassMeans=0.1965999901,0.6074249744,0.08072499186,0.05892499164,
0.4636749625,0.3251250386,0.55400002,0.5070499182,0.6223250031,
0.3915250301,0.7695249915,0.8010498881
FeatureFlags=1,1,1,1
Trained=TRUE
Built=TRUE
```

Regression Tool

Chapter 7.6

Overview

The Regression tool is a prediction tool that uses multiple linear regression, a statistical technique, to model your data.

Note: Multiple Linear Regression can be used for prediction problems only.

This chapter provides the following information:

*   Explains the ideas behind multiple linear regression

*   Explains how to use the Regression tool

Note: The Regression tool does not have a dialog box.

What Is Multiple Linear Regression?

Given a training set of noisy data, multiple regression analysis finds a functional relationship between the input variables or attributes and the output. Once this relationship is found, a predicted output for a new set of input variables, not in the original training set, can be computed.

Multiple regression makes two critical assumptions. The first is that the outputs and the inputs are linearly related. The second is that there is no interaction between the input variables.

If the output *Y* is linked to the data inputs *U, V...* then, assuming

```
Y = a + bU + cV +...
```

it is possible to calculate values for *a, b, c,...*

and to predict the values of new, unknown outputs.

When the data cannot be fitted exactly to an equation of this type, an approximation of the equation gives predictions

Y', where

```
Y' = a + bV +cV...
```

and

```
Y = a + bV + cV +...+ e
```

where *e* is a measure of the error.

By minimizing the error using regression techniques, a best-fit equation can be reached.

Using the Regression Tool

To train the Multiple Linear Regression tool:

- From the Multiple Linear Regression menu, choose **Train**.

Multiple Regression Coefficients

When a Multiple Regression object has been trained, the coefficients that have been chosen can be viewed.

To view the Multiple Regression coefficients:

- From the Multiple Linear Regression menu, choose **Print**.

Saved Settings

As explained in Appendix I, a Neural Connection application is saved as a text file with an *.nni* extension. Within the file, each tool has its own text commands that set up the tool when it is loaded into Neural Connection. Some of these can be altered in text form, but it is strongly recommended that any changes be made using Neural Connection's workspace.

The application can be loaded into Neural Connection by using the **Open** command on the File menu.

An example of a saved Multiple Linear Regression tool is given below. Some of the text has been omitted, indicated by the elipses (...).

```
[Multiple Regression]
.Name=Regr1
.GridX=12
.GridY=21
Version="1.0"
ObjectiveFunction="Unknown"
NumInputs=41
NumTargets=1
NumRows=43
NumCols=43
NumCells=946
XVector=0,0,0,0,0,0,0,0,0,0,0,0,0,0,0,0,0,0,0,0,0,0,0,0,
0,0,0,0,0,0,0,0,0,0,0,0,0,0,0,0,-0.800916276943450689
DKMatrix0=983840,17.596433363148474172,0.077518702228004457422,-
5.6272940722068671704,12.437175760286233839
DKMatrix5=0.18483696536022109491,0.031645389494226690286,
0.0065498455033338775014,0.014277728085867625457,
0.016985485444787742915
...
DKMatrix940=2.4668727005971347388e-027,-0.015592363446858792733,
-1554841999230.4030762,1.1280871175177121482e-028,
76851636814396.734375
DKMatrix945=0
Trained=TRUE
Built=TRUE
```

Principal Component Analysis Tool

Chapter 7.7

Overview

Principal Component Analysis is a useful tool for reducing the overspecification of data. It uses statistical techniques to produce a less complex data set that represents your problem.

The Principal Component Analysis tool is an unsupervised technique and does not require that your data contain target answers.

This chapter provides the following information:

- Explains the ideas behind principal component analysis

- Explains how to use the Principal Component Analysis tool

What Is Principal Component Analysis?

By choosing a set of orthogonal vectors (principal components) that account for as much of the data variance as possible, the dimensionality of your data can be reduced. For example, a data set with 10 separate data fields might be well-represented by only five principal components, halving the number of variables while retaining almost all the information. Obviously, further analysis of the data will then be considerably simpler.

The principal components are derived from the eigenvalues and eigenvectors of the correlation matrix of the data set. Before the principal components can be generated, the correlation matrix must be calculated.

Using the Principal Component Analysis Tool

To train the Principal Component Analysis tool:

• From the Principal Component Analysis menu, choose **Train**.

Selecting the Principal Components

Principal components are chosen in order; the first is chosen to be along the direction with the maximum variance in the data, the second to be along the direction that has the maximum data variance in the subspace orthogonal to the first principal component, and so on. The lower the order of the principal component, the lower the variance of the data along the component.

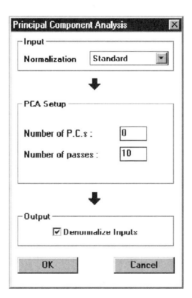

The Principal Component Analysis dialog box

Neural Connection allows you to specify the number of principal components into which your data will be separated. You can specify any number of principal components up to the number of data fields in your data set.

To select the number of principal components:

1. From the Principal Component Analysis menu, choose **Dialog**.

2. In the **Number of P.C.s** field, type the number of Principal Components required.

3. Click **OK**.

When it is calculating the correlation matrix, the Principal Component Analysis tool uses an iterative technique known as *Oja's method*. This calculates the matrix by adjusting a set of parameters after each record is shown to it. When a stable set of parameters has been found, these give the correlation matrix. For more information see Appendix III, Algorithms.

In order to ensure that stable parameters have been found, it is important to pass the data through the algorithm a sufficient number of times. This is done by setting the number of passes.

To set the number of passes:

1. From the Principal Component Analysis menu, choose **Dialog**.

2. In the **Number of passes** field, type the number of passes required.

3. Click **OK**.

Normalization

Data normalization ensures that each input contributes equally to the decision or prediction made by the network.

If the input values were not normalized, an input that varied over the range 100 to 110 would be far more significant than one that varied over the range 1.0 to 2.0. In fact, the first input, although of greater absolute magnitude, varies by only 10%, while the second varies by 100%.

To normalize incoming data:

1. From the Principal Component Analysis menu, choose **Dialog**.

2. Select **Normalize incoming data**.

3. Click **OK**.

To de-normalize outgoing data:

1. From the Principal Component Analysis menu, choose **Dialog**.

2. Select **De-normalize outgoing data**.

3. Click **OK**.

Saved Settings

As explained in Appendix I, a Neural Connection application is saved as a text file with an *.nni* extension. Within the file, each tool has its own text commands that set up the tool when it is loaded into Neural Connection. Some of these can be altered in text form, but it is strongly recommended that any changes be made using Neural Connection's workspace.

The application can be loaded into Neural Connection by using the **Open** command on the File menu.

An example of a saved Principal Component Analysis tool is given below. Some of the text has been omitted, indicated by the elipses (…).

```
[Principal Component Analysis]
.Name=PCA1
.GridX=15
.GridY=7
Version="1.0"
NormInputs="Standard"
NormTargets="Standard"
NumPCs=8
StopEpochs=10
Invert=FALSE
InvertName=""
NumInputs=8
PrincipleComponents=8,8,8,7.060296059,0.7943732142,0.05114227161,
0.04291282594,0.01647787727,0.01578648761,0.01084791683,
0.008057758212,7.99985218,8
InputNorm=8,225,8,0.7268922925,0.6406063437,0.4318801165,
0.7523679137,0.7515919805,0.750815928,0.7500399351,0.7492639422
…
TargetNorm=8,225,8,1.849496126,-0.7222058773,-0.01205997635,
0.00697185006,-0.03823663294,-0.004977145698,0.0002191606618,
…
Iteration=2251
Built=TRUE
Trained=TRUE
Ranges1=4.467066765,-1.447189093
Ranges2=-0.6305032969,-0.8768503666
…
Ranges8=0.000456858048,0.0004541459202
VectorColumn1=8,0.3504112065,0.4498835802,0.5036413074,
0.2777283788,0.2851477563,0.2909699082,0.2960070968,0.3007261455
VectorColumn2=8,-0.1078587994,0.3089693785,0.6615517735,
0.3419090211,-0.32094872,-0.3009890914,-0.280267477,-0.2572923899
…
VectorColumn8=8,-0.01580525748,-0.008872262202,0.006360185798,
0.02709426731,-0.2176928818,0.5905920863,-0.7050483227,
0.3249839544
```

Filter Tools

Chapter 8

Overview

Filter tools manipulate data in different ways in order to allow you to produce the best solution to your problem. Neural Connection has four filter tools:

- The Filter tool, discussed in Chapter 8.1

- The Combiner tool, discussed in Chapter 8.2

- The Simulator tool, discussed in Chapter 8.3

- The Time Series Window, discussed in Chapter 8.4

Filter Tool

Chapter 8.1

Overview

The Filter tool can enable or disable fields of data, give an analysis of the distribution of a data field, and scale data fields using mathematical functions.

This chapter provides the following information:

- Gives an overview of how the Filter tool can be useful

- Explains how to use the Filter tool to preprocess data

- Explains how to use the Filter tool to analyze data

Why Use a Filter Tool?

It is often important to preprocess input data when using a modeling and forecasting tool and the Filter tool allows you to do this. Neural networks work best when the input data they are using have a uniform distribution and when the data are presented so that significant areas have the highest definition. This is because of the way in which the neurons in a neural network operate. The output of a neuron is normalized so that it is approximately linear over the range of data. However, this can result in a loss of definition for data that are at the extremes of the data range.

Unfortunately, in real problems data are rarely uniformly distributed. For example, when looking at a distribution of salaries in order to make a decision about lending, the important data range is that around the cut-off point for lending. It is unlikely that you would lend to people far below this point or that you would not lend to someone far above it.

It is a general rule that applications work best when you can expand the data around which decisions are made. If a mathematical function exists that emphasizes this part of your data, applying the function to your data will improve your application's performance.

To help you to visualize how a mathematical function will transform your data, the Filter tool can perform simple analysis of the distribution of your data both before and after transformation.

The Filter tool can be used to enable or disable fields of input data for use by successor objects. This allows you to check the importance of a field of data to your problem without having to remove it from the training and test files.

Preprocessing Data

The Filter tool can preprocess input data fields in two ways. It can select the data fields used by the application and it can weight the data in the data fields.

Selecting Data Fields

Data fields can be switched on or off by the filter. When they are selected, the Filter passes them to successor objects when requested. When they are not selected, the data are unavailable to successor objects.

To switch a data field on or off:

1. From the Filter menu, choose **Dialog**.

2. In the Filter dialog box, click the **Use State** cell of the column of the data field whose state you want to change.

3. Click the drop-down list next to the text entry field in the top left hand corner of the Filter dialog box.

4. Select the state to which you want to change the field (**Yes** or **No**).

5. Click **OK**.

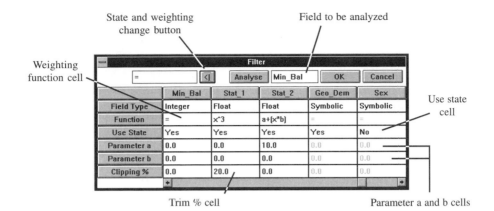

The Filter Dialog Box

Weighting Data

Data can be weighted in several ways in order to maximize their usefulness to the application. These weightings cannot be used with symbolic data, nor can logarithms or natural logarithms be used with integer data.

Note: If a data field contains a zero entry or a negative entry, you cannot weight it using a logarithm or a natural logarithm.

To weight data fields:

1. From the Filter menu, choose **Dialog**.

2. In the Filter dialog box, click the **Function** cell of the data field whose weighting you want to change.

3. To access the weighting functions, click the drop-down list next to the text entry field in the top left of the window.

4. To change the weighting, select the desired function.

5. Click **OK**.

Many of the functions used allow you to set two parameters, **a** and **b**.

To set parameter **a** or **b**:

1. From the Filter menu, choose **Dialog**.

2. In the Filter window click the **Parameter a** or **Parameter b** cell of the data field whose function parameters you want to change.

3. In the text entry field in the top left of the window, type the desired value.

4. Click **OK**.

The following symbols are used for various functions:

Function	Symbol	Explanation
Value	=	The field is not weighted.
Square	^2	Elements in the field are squared.
Cube	^3	Elements in the field are cubed.
Square-Root Sqrt	(x)	Elements in the field have their square roots taken.

Note: *When using this function,* x *cannot take a negative value.*

Reciprocal	1/(x+a)	Elements in the field have a constant, **a**, added to them and the reciprocal is then taken.

Note: *When using this function,* ***x+a*** *can not equal 0.*

Linear	a+(x*b)	Elements in the field are multiplied by a constant, **b**, and added to a constant, **a**.

Note: *When using this function the value of* ***x*b*** *may exceed the mathematical limits of the system.*

Limit	a<=x<=b	**Limit** is a limiting function. If **a** is less than **b**, an element that is below **a** or above **b** is set to 0; otherwise, it is set to 1.
		If **a** is greater than **b**, an element that is below **b** or above **a** is set to 1; otherwise, it is set to 0.
Exponential	Exp(x)	**E** raised to the power of the element.

Note: *When using this function the value of* e^x *may exceed the mathematical limits of the system.*

Function	Symbol	Explanation
Natural Logarithm	**ln(x+a)**	The element is added to a constant and the natural logarithm is taken.

Note: When using this function x+a must be greater than 0.

Logarithm of Quotient	**ln((x-a)/(b-x))**	The quotient of the element is taken using constants **a** and **b**. The natural logarithm of this quotient is then taken.

Note: When using this function (x-a)/(b-x) must be greater than 0, and b-x must not equal 0.

Base 10 Logarithm	**log(x+a)**	A constant is added to the element and the base 10 logarithm is taken.

Note: When using this function x+a must be greater than 0.

ArcSin Square Root	**asin(sqrt(x))**	The square root of the element is taken; then the arcsine taken.

Note: When using this function x must be greater than 0 and less than 1.

Box-Cox Transformation	**((x+a)^b-1)/b**	A Box-Cox transformation is applied to the element.

Note: When using this function the value of (x+a)b may exceed the mathematical limits of the system.

Trimming

Trimming a data field reduces the range of the data set. When the data field is trimmed, a percentage of the data field at the top and bottom of its range is set to a fixed value, which is the value of the data field at the extremes of the new range. The maximum level of trim allowed is 50%.

To trim a data field:

1. From the Filter menu, choose **Dialog**
2. In the Filter dialog box select the **Clipping %** cell of the data field whose trim you want to change.
3. In the text entry field in the top left of the window, type the desired level of trim.
4. Click **OK**.

Analysis

Neural Connection allows simple analysis of data fields.

To analyze a data field:

1. From the Filter menu, choose **Dialog**.

2. In the Filter dialog box, click the name of the data field you want to analyze.

3. Click **Analyze**.

4. Click **OK**.

The Filter analysis window shows a number of statistical measures and a histogram of the distribution of the data field across its range. The range is divided into 10 equal bins.

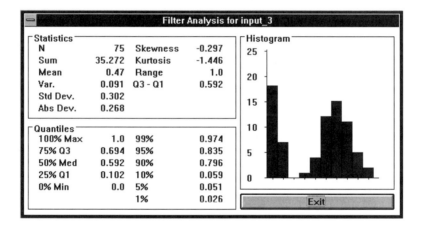

Filter analysis window

Note: *When analyzing symbolic data, a histogram of the distribution of examples is shown together with a color code chart for the classes and the total number of examples in each class. Statistical measures are not shown.*

The statistical measures used include:

N	The number of elements in the data field.
Sum	The sum of the elements in the data field.
Mean	The mean value of elements in the data field.
Var	The variance of elements in the data field from the mean.
Std Dev	The standard deviation of elements in the field from the mean.
Abs Dev	The absolute deviation of elements in the field from the mean.
Skewness	The *skewness* is a measure of the tendency of the deviations from the mean to be larger in one direction than in the other. A positive value of skewness indicates that the data are skewed to the right, while a negative value of skewness indicates that the data are skewed to the left.
Kurtosis	*Kurtosis* is a measure of the heaviness of the tails of a data distribution. It is standardized so that a normal distribution has a kurtosis of 0.
Range	The range over which the data are distributed.
	The difference between the third quartile and the second quartile (see *quantiles* below).
Quantiles	A *quantile* is a value below which the fraction of the data set specified in the quantile can be found. The *quartiles* are the quantiles taken at 25%, 50%, and 75% of the data set.

Saved Settings

As explained in Appendix I, a Neural Connection application is saved as a text file with an *.nni* extension. Within the file, each tool has its own text commands that set up the tool when it is loaded into Neural Connection. Some of these can be altered in text form, but it is strongly recommended that any changes be made using Neural Connection's workspace.

The application can be loaded into Neural Connection by using the **Open** command on the File menu.

An example of a saved Filter tool is shown below:

```
[Filter]
.Name=Filter1
.GridX=10
.GridY=16
Version="1.0"
NumInputs=4
Name1="var_0001"
Type1=FLOAT
Name2="var_0002"
Type2=FLOAT
Name3="var_0003"
Type3=FLOAT
Name4="var_0004"
Type4=FLOAT
In1="Value",FALSE,0,0,0
In2="Cube",TRUE,2,0,2
In3="Value",TRUE,0,0,0
In4="LnQuotient",TRUE,0.5,0.8000000119,0
```

Combiner Tool

Chapter 8.2

Overview

The Combiner tool is the way that you join different data paths in Neural Connection.

This chapter provides the following information:

- Explains why the Combiner tool is useful
- Explains how to use the Combiner tool

Note: The Combiner tool does not have a dialog box.

Why Use a Combiner Tool?

The Combiner tool allows you to combine the output from two or more distinct network objects into a single output, thus enabling the creation of complex application topologies.

Using a Combiner Tool

To use the Combiner tool:

1. Connect the tools whose outputs you want to merge to the Combiner object.
2. Connect the Combiner to the tool to which you want to pass the merged data.

Data that are fed through a Combiner are not altered by it.

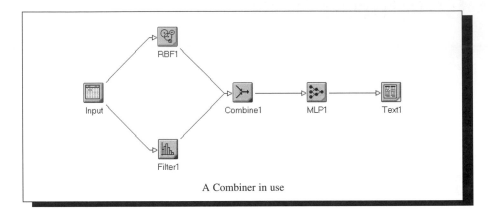

A Combiner in use

If an application is run from a tool downstream from a Combiner, all the objects upstream from it will be automatically trained before data are passed through the application.

Connections to and from the Combiner are made in the usual way.

Note: *The Combiner cannot be used to create a feedback loop*

Saved Settings

As explained in Appendix I, a Neural Connection application is saved as a text file with an *.nni* extension. Within the file, each tool has its own text commands that set up the tool when it is loaded into Neural Connection. Some of these can be altered in text form, but it is strongly recommended that any changes be made using Neural Connection's workspace.

The application can be loaded into Neural Connection by using the **Open** command on the File menu.

An example of a saved Combiner tool is shown below:

```
[Network Combiner]
.Name=Combine2
.GridX=17
.GridY=14
Version="1.0"
NumInputs=2
```

Simulator Tool

Chapter 8.3

Overview

The Simulator tool produces a continuous set of data to model your problem. It can produce output for any two of your input fields. The output can be as fine or coarse as necessary.

The Simulator tool *must* be used with the What If? tool and the Graphics Output tool.

This chapter provides the following information:

* Explains why the Simulator tool is useful

* Explains how to use the Simulator tool to produce a continuous data set

Why Use the Simulator Tool?

When the output of a modeling tool is plotted against the values of two input fields, the surface that is plotted is the function that links the input field values and the output of the modeling tool. If the model is giving good results, it is an approximation of a function that links the input field values and the output in the real data. However, real test data would probably be irregularly scattered over the range of the data and plotting them in this way would give only a sparse graph.

To overcome this problem, the Simulator creates a pseudo test file, in which the values of the input fields in which you are interested are varied over their entire ranges while the other input fields are fixed at their mean values. This pseudo test file is then passed on to the modeling tool, which is trained on the real data, and a results file is produced that can be passed on to the Graphics Output or the What If? tool.

Using the Simulator Tool

The Simulator tool must be placed upstream of the modeling tool from which you want to plot results.

To activate the Simulator tool:

1. From the Simulator menu, choose **Dialog**.

2. In the Simulator box, select **Enabled.**

3. Click **OK**.

You must indicate which of the input fields you want to use and the increments at which the pseudo test data are to be created.

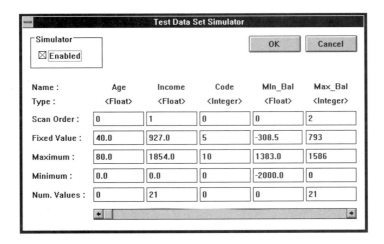

The Simulator Dialog window

To select the input fields to be simulated:

1. From the Simulator menu, choose **Dialog**.

2. In the **Scan Order** boxes below the input fields you want to simulate, type **1** and **2**.

3. Click **OK**.

To choose the number of increments:

1. From the Simulator menu, choose **Dialog**.

2. In the **Num. Values** boxes below the input fields you have selected, type the number of increments required.

3. Click **OK**.

Note: *Input fields that you do not use are fixed at their mean value. If another value would be more appropriate, it can be entered in the **Fixed Value** box for that input.*

Saved Settings

As explained in Appendix I, a Neural Connection application is saved as a text file with an *.nni* extension. Within the file, each tool has its own text commands that set up the tool when it is loaded into Neural Connection. Some of these can be altered in text form, but it is strongly recommended that any changes be made using Neural Connection's workspace.

The application can be loaded into Neural Connection by using the **Open** command on the File menu.

An example of a saved Simulator tool is shown below:

```
[Test Data Simulator]
.Name=Sim2
.GridX=20
.GridY=14
Version="1.0"
NumInputs=2
InputCol1="RBF4",FLOAT
InputCol2="RBF5",FLOAT
Active=FALSE
NumRecords=441
NumVarColumns=2
VDFValid=TRUE
Out1=1,0.5,"",1,0,21
Out2=2,0.5,"",1,0,21
Enabled=TRUE
```

Time Series Window

Chapter 8.4

Overview

The Time Series Window allows you to use windowing techniques to concatenate a time series before processing it.

This chapter provides the following information:

- Explains why the Time Series Window is useful

- Introduces the ideas of windowing a time series and multistep ahead prediction

- Explains how to use the Time Series Window to produce a window from time series data

- Explains how to set up single or multistep ahead prediction

Why Use the Time Series Window?

A time series database usually contains one or more input columns, each of which represents a feature that was recorded at time intervals. Each line in the database represents values recorded at the same time. Usually these files do not contain target values since the targets, or forecast variables, are to be found in the subsequent values in the time series.

Windowing is a technique that assumes that the sequence of values in one window is related to a following sequence and that, although this relationship is unknown, it is fully defined within the data set.

The Time Series Window also allows two types of prediction to take place, *single step* prediction and *multistep* prediction. In single step prediction, an application predicts the next value, or event, in a time series ($t+1$) and the window steps forward ($t \rightarrow t+1$). A new prediction is then made using the actual value at $t+1$, not the previously predicted one. There is no feedback in single step prediction.

In multistep prediction, the prediction for $t+1$ is fed back into the application as an input and a new output ($t+2$) is generated. This in turn is fed back into the application as an input. Multistep prediction thus allows you to predict results even after you have run out of actual data in the test set and so gives you the ability to produce long range forecasts.

Using the Time Series Window

The Time Series Window acts as a substitute input tool. It should be placed upstream of any modeling tools that need to use a windowing technique on time series data.

Note: For information on randomizing time series windowed data, please see Chapter 5.1, Data Input Tool.

Selecting the Prediction Technique

The Time Series Window can be set to either single step or multistep prediction.

To select single step prediction:

1. From the Time Series Window menu, choose **Dialog**.

2. In the Prediction Technique group, select **Single Step Prediction.**

3. Click **OK**.

Multistep prediction must be run from a specified output tool. The number of time steps it should predict from its starting point must also be selected.

To select multistep prediction:

1. From the Time Series Window menu, choose **Dialog**.

2. In the Prediction Technique group, select **Multi-Step Prediction.**

3. In the **No. of Look Ahead Steps** field, type the number of time steps to predict ahead.

4. In the **Name of Active Output** field, type the name of the output tool from which the Time Series Window application will be run. Notice that the Time Series Window is case sensitive, so you must be sure that the name is typed in the correct case. For example, *Forward* is different from *forward*.

5. Click **OK**.

Creating the Window

The window you create in the Time Series Window defines the data set on which any subsequent tools will operate. The window creates both the inputs and the target outputs for any subsequent processing.

Creation of the window occurs in two parts--the inputs window and the forecast window.

Each field can be given a window size and a window resolution for both the input variables and the forecast variables, the target outputs. *Window size* gives the number of elements in that field in the window. *Window resolution* gives the spacing of the elements in that field in the window, in number of time steps.

Note: *When using multistep prediction, some care must be taken when setting the window size. The window resolution, window size, and step size must be consistent, as the Time Series Window needs to use data generated from the target window in future inputs windows.*

Note: *If you do not want to use an input field in either the input or forecast window you can set the window size to 0.*

To create an inputs window:

1. From the Time Series Window menu, choose **Dialog**.

2. In the fields provided for the inputs of each input field, type the desired **Window Size** and **Window Resolution**.

3. Click **OK**.

Example 1

If you wanted to set the following window from this time series, you would set up the dialog box as follows:

```
time series data
t-3    1      3      -2
t-2    2      5      -1
t-1    3      7       0                    input window
t      4      9       1      ->            4, 7, 9, -2, 1
t+1    5     11       2
t+2    6     13       2
t+3    7     12       1
t+4    8     11       0
t+5    9     10      -1
```

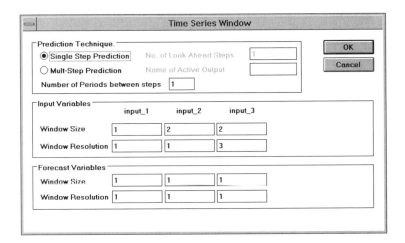

The Time Series Window dialog window: Example 1

To create a forecast window:

1. From the Time Series Window menu, choose **Dialog**.

2. In the fields provided for the forecasts of each input field, type the desired **Window Size** and **Window Resolution**.

3. Click **OK**.

Example 2

If you wanted to set the following forecast window from this time series, you would set up the dialog box as follows:

```
time series data
t-3     1     3     -2
t-2     2     5     -1
t-1     3     7      0
t       4     9      1                    forecast window
t+1     5    11      2     ->             11, 2, 2
t+2     6    13      2
t+3     7    12      1
t+4     8    11      0
t+5     9    10     -1
```

In this example we do not want to use the first input column as a target, so we have set the target window size for that column to 0.

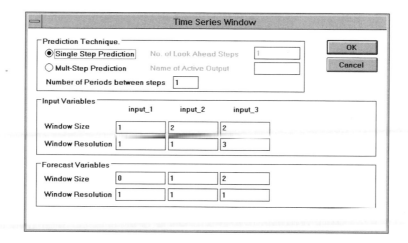

The Time Series Window dialog window: Example 2

The Step Size

The step size sets the number of time steps to move the window when producing inputs and forecast variables.

To set the step size:

1. From the Time Series Window menu, choose **Dialog**.

2. In the Prediction Technique group's **Number of Periods between steps** field, type the desired step size.

3. Click **OK**.

Saved Settings

As explained in Appendix I, a Neural Connection application is saved as a text file with an *.nni* extension. Within the file, each tool has its own text commands that set up the tool when it is loaded into Neural Connection. Some of these can be altered in text form, but it is strongly recommended that any changes be made using Neural Connection's workspace.

The application can be loaded into Neural Connection by using the **Open** command on the File menu.

An example of a saved Time Series Window tool is shown below:

```
[Time Series Window]
.Name=TSW1
.GridX=11
.GridY=9
Version="1.0"
OgTrainRecs=201
OgValidRecs=24
OgCombRecs=226
OgRunRecs=25
ProblemType=UNKNOWN
MultiStepSeq=0
NumInputs=9
OldPosition=0
InputCol1="var_0001",FLOAT
InputCol2="var_0002",FLOAT
InputCol3="var_0003",FLOAT
InputCol4="var_0004",FLOAT
InputCol5="var_0005",FLOAT
InputCol6="var_0006",FLOAT
InputCol7="var_0007",FLOAT
InputCol8="var_0008",FLOAT
InputCol9="var_0009",FLOAT
Active=FALSE
MaxInputWindow=1
```

```
MaxTargetWindow=1
FirstPass=TRUE
AssignType=1
RandomSeed=12345
NumBlocks=1
StepPeriod=1
Prediction="Single"
LookAhead=1
TSW1=1,1,0,1
TSW2=1,1,0,1
TSW3=1,1,0,1
TSW4=1,1,0,1
TSW5=1,1,0,1
TSW6=1,1,0,1
TSW7=1,1,0,1
TSW8=1,1,0,1
TSW9=0,1,1,1
ActiveOutput=""
```

Appendixes

Overview

There are four appendixes that cover the following subjects:

Appendix I, Script Language   Information on saved files and how to write a NetAgent language file

Appendix II, SPSS File Conversion   How SPSS for Windows files are interpreted when opened in the Data Input tool and how they are written out by the Text Output tool

Appendix III, Algorithms   A guide to the algorithms used in the Neural Connection tools

Appendix IV, General Reference   The history of the development of neural computing

Saved Applications and the Script Language

Appendix I

Overview

Neural Connection saves applications in a format that can be read using any text editor. This enables you to examine the applications that you have built and extract the weights from the neural networks. The .nni language, in which applications are saved, contains information on the tools and their parameters and on the topology connecting the tools. It also contains information on the way that tools have been trained in a saved network.

Neural Connection also has a scripting language. The NetAgent language trains and runs the application. It allows an application to be run, allows user interaction, and enables comments to be displayed while the application trains and runs.

This appendix provides the following information:

- Explains how to understand a saved file

- Explains how to write a NetAgent language file

- Gives details and syntax for the NetAgent language commands

Saved Applications *(.nni)*

Saved application files are ASCII text files that have been saved with an *.nni* extension. You can use Neural Connection to generate an *.nni* file by saving your application.

Each tool has its own set of commands (described below). The type of tool appears in square brackets ([ ]) at the start of the commands relating to that tool, followed by its position on the workspace.

Some commands are accompanied by a single parameter, while others require a named function.

Saved application files follow a few rules:

- They can have only one command per line.

- A blank line must be left between the commands of different tools.

- One and only one topology section must be included, specifying the connections between tools.

- Comments can be inserted by preceding them with an exclamation mark.

Saved application files may contain any number of tool declarations, each of which defines the type, name, and position of the tool. Multiple tools of the same type must be identified by different tool names.

To load a saved application file:

1. To clear the workspace, from the File menu choose **New**.

2. From the File menu, choose **Open**.

3. Either click a file, or type the name and path of the file in the filename box.

4. Click **OK**.

Tool Commands

Each tool has its own set of parameters. Some parameters should not be edited. Others, related to the tool's adjustable parameters, may be edited by hand within the *.nni* file, although this is not recommended (any changeable parameters can be altered using Neural Connection's workspace and saved in the normal way). When editing, tools should be named by specifying a name in the **.Name =** field and must be given a position on the workspace by using the **.GridX =** and **.GridY =** fields.

Examples of the .nni language commands that show the saved settings for each type of tool appear at the end of that tool's chapter.

The Application Topology

Every saved file must describe the connections between tools and the order in which they are connected. This is done in the topology section. The start of a topology section within a saved file is identified by **[Topology]**.

The topology is specified connection by connection, using **->** to indicate a connection from the left hand tool to the right hand tool. Tools must be referred to by their name, not by their type. For example:

```
[Topology]
Source -> PCA
Source -> Sim
Source -> Flt
PCA -> RBF
RBF -> TextOutput
```

NetAgent Language

The NetAgent Language allows an application to be run with little or no interaction from the user. Situations in which this could be useful include:

- Running in batch mode, for running a set of experiments overnight

- Running in demonstration mode, for use at a trade show

- Running as an end use application, by operators who have not been involved in developing the application

To load a NetAgent file:

1. To clear the workspace, from the File menu choose **New**.

2. From the Options menu, choose **NetAgent**.

3. Either click a **NetAgent** file, or type the name and path of the file in the filename box.

4. Click **OK**.

The following rules apply:

- The NetAgent file must be an ASCII text file that contains one command per line, with no blank lines.

- No line in the NetAgent file may exceed 80 characters.

- Certain commands must be accompanied by a single parameter. No command takes more than one parameter.

- To be recognized by Neural Connection, NetAgent language files must be saved with an *.agt* extension.

The application exits immediately under the following conditions:

- A specified command is unknown.

- A mandatory parameter is missing or invalid.

- Executing a command causes an error in the application.

The commands in a NetAgent file are carried out in order. After the last command in the file has been executed, control returns to the user, who can then use the application normally (unless the **Quit** command has caused the application to close down).

NetAgent Language Commands

The commands available in the NetAgent language are described below.

Load	**Load** *<file.nni>* loads a saved application. This command can be used only when no tools have been placed on the workspace. If an application has already been loaded using LoadTask or Load, the **Reset** command must be used before LoadTask can be used.
SaveTask	**SaveTask** saves the current application under the name specified by **SaveTaskName**. If no name has been specified, the application is saved as *AGTTASK1.NNT*.
SaveTaskName	**SaveTaskName** *<name>* sets the name under which an application is saved.
IncrTaskName	**IncrTaskName** increments the name under which an application is saved by one. For example, an application named *mail1.nni* becomes *mail2.nni,* etc.
Reset	**Reset** has the same effect as choosing **New** from the File menu.
Quit	**Quit** exits the current NetAgent script and returns to the workspace.

Train	**Train** *<instance name>* trains a specified Network tool instance. The instance must exist and the name specified must match that given to the instance in the saved application file.
Run	**Run** *<instance name>* runs an specified instance of an Output tool. The instance must exist and the name specified must match that given to the instance in the saved application file.
Print	**Print** *<instance name>* displays the data body of an instance. The instance must exist and the name specified must match that given to the instance in the saved application file.
Dialog	**Dialog** *<instance name>* displays the dialog box of the specified tool instance. If the tool does not support a dialog box, nothing happens.

*Note: Once the dialog box appears, control returns to the user, who must click either **OK** or **Cancel** in the box in order to resume execution of the NetAgent file script.*

Textoff	**Textoff** switches off the text display in the application window, returning the user to the icon display; a text display must be active before this command is used.
Graphoff	**Graphoff** switches off the graphics display in the application window, returning the user to the icon display; a graphics display must be active before this command is used.
Box	**Box** *<On/Off>* displays or hides the NetAgent dialog box. It does not cause an error to change the state of the box to the state that it's already in.
Wait	**Wait** *<seconds>* waits until the user clicks either **Continue** or **Cancel** in the NetAgent dialog box or until the specified number of seconds has elapsed (whichever happens sooner). If the user clicks **Cancel**, Neural Connection stops running the NetAgent file and the user can use the application normally. If either the user clicks **Continue** or the specified number of seconds elapses without the user clicking either button, then Neural Connection moves on to the next command in the NetAgent file. If the number of seconds is set to zero, **Neural Connection** does not proceed until one of the buttons is clicked.

Although this command is primarily intended for use in conjunction with the NetAgent dialog box, it can also be used to cause a timed delay when the box is off. However, setting **Wait** to zero seconds while the box is off crashes the program since neither button is available to be pressed.

Message   **Message1** *<message>* - Displays a message on the first line of the NetAgent dialog box. Specifying *<message>* as *XXX* causes the line to be cleared.

Message2 *<message>* - Displays a message on the second line of the NetAgent dialog box.

Note: *The NetAgent dialog box must be displayed before issuing a **Message1** or **Message2** command. When starting to interpret the NetAgent script, the box is off (hidden) by default.*

Loop   **Loop** *<count>* causes the commands that follow (up until the next Endloop command) to be executed in a loop. The *<count>* parameter specifies how many times to go round the loop; if zero is specified, the loop iterates forever. Loops may be nested up to a depth of 10 loops.

Endloop   **Endloop** marks the end of the loop that started with the last Loop command encountered.

Question   **Question** allows an input to the application from NetAgent. The Question command can be used in three ways:

- **Question**

    Displays a dialog box with **Continue** and **Quit** buttons. To continue the NetAgent script, **Continue** must be clicked.

- **Question name$**

    Displays a dialog box with a text edit field and **Continue** and **Quit** buttons. When **Continue** is clicked, the text in the text edit field is stored as the variable name$.

- **Question name$ "Text1" "Text2" "Text3"**

    Displays a dialog box with radio buttons for each of the options specified and **Continue** and **Quit** buttons. Beside each button is the label specified (for example *"Text1"*). When **Continue** is clicked, the label of the selected radio button is stored as the variable name$.

IfEqual   **IfEqual** checks a value against that of a variable. This is most usually used with a **Goto** statement. For example:

IfEqual name$ "Yes" Goto correct

where *correct* is a label.

Goto	**Goto** moves the script directly to a named label
\<label\>:	**\<label\>:** defines a named label
name$	variable format
!	**!** is a comment delimiter

SPSS File Conversion

Appendix II

Overview

This appendix provides the following information:

- Gives details of how SPSS files are read into the Data Input tool

- Gives details of how the Data Input and Text Output tools write SPSS files

Importing Data

Neural Connection has only three data types: numeric (floating point), integer, and symbolic. Consequently many SPSS data types have to be converted when a file is read into the Data Input tool.

When reading SPSS data files, Neural Connection makes the following conversions:

SPSS data	Neural Connection data
Numeric	Numeric
Comma	Numeric
Dot	Numeric
Scientific	Numeric
Date	Numeric
Dollar	Numeric
Custom Currency	Numeric
String	Symbolic

The following section lists the attributes of SPSS *.sav* files that Neural Connection can load.

Compression	Neural Connection can read both compressed and uncompressed SPSS data.
Dates	Dates are handled by using the numeric translation written by SPSS. No translation is performed by Neural Connection. This does not always produce the best format for analysis (see the *Applications Guide*).
Field Type	Fields are translated to the nearest Neural Connection field type as shown above.
Field Width	There is no set field width within Neural Connection, so this attribute is not imported.
Justification	All numeric and integer fields in Neural Connection are right justified, and all symbolic fields are left justified.
Numerical Definition	Numerical values in Neural Connection are stored as floating point data, and definition is limited by this.
Split Variables	Split variables are not handled by Neural Connection.
Text	There is a maximum width of 13 characters for Neural Connection symbolic data. Any text field wider than 13 characters is truncated to 13 characters.
User Missing	All user-defined missing values are translated as "missing."
Weighting Variables	Weighting variables are not handled by Neural Connection.

Note: *If the field headers are saved to a file that is loaded into Neural Connection, all field types are read as symbolic. Any numerics encountered are added to the list of inconsistencies. This is done deliberately, to highlight the possibility of a numeric being accidentally entered in a symbolic field. See Chapter 5.1, Data Input Tool.*

Exporting Data

Neural Connection has only three data types: numeric (floating point), integer, and symbolic. Consequently, when the Data Input or Text Output tool writes to an SPSS file, many field types are not used.

When writing SPSS data files Neural Connection makes the following conversions:

Neural Connection data	SPSS data
Numeric	Numeric
Integer	Numeric
Symbolic	String

The following section lists the attributes of SPSS *.sav* files that Neural Connection can write.

Compression
Neural Connection writes only uncompressed SPSS data files.

Field Type
Fields are translated to the field types shown above.

Field Width
There is no set field width within Neural Connection, so this attribute is not exported.

Invalid Entries in the Spreadsheet Input Tool
Neural Connection prevents the saving of files from the Data Input tool if the list of inconsistencies contains invalid entries. This list is created when data are loaded into the Data Input tool. For more information, see Chapter 5.1, Data Input Tool.

Justification
All numeric and integer fields in Neural Connection are right justified; all symbolic fields are left justified.

Text
There is a maximum width of 13 characters for Neural Connection symbolic data. Text is written out with a limit of 13 characters.

User Missing
Missing values cannot be passed to the Text Output tool, so no missing values can be written. When an SPSS file is saved from the Data Input tool, missing values are written correctly.

Algorithms

Appendix III

Overview

This appendix is an introduction to the algorithms used in Neural Connection. It has been designed to give an insight into the processes that take place in the modeling and forecasting tools used in the program. The algorithms used in each modeling and forecasting tool are examined in separate sections. For a more detailed description of neural networks, refer to a technical reference book.

The algorithms described are based on the assumption that the data set shown to the application has been broken into three parts—the training, validation, and test data sets. These sets have clearly defined uses within the neural networks, but they also allow the classical statistical techniques to differentiate clearly between the data used to build a model, and the data that are applied to the model to produce an output.

For a full description of the training, validation, and test data sets, see Chapter 5.

Closest Class Mean Classifier

This section provides the following information:

- Outlines the closest class means method
- Shows a sample calculation using the method

Method

Closest class means classification is a classical statistical technique that places examples in one of a series of predefined classes.

The closest class means algorithm determines class membership in a very straightforward way. An example is assigned to a class with the smallest distance between the example and the center of the class. The class centers are calculated from the training data presented to the application.

The classes are defined in the targets that are presented in the training data set. This means that only classes that are present in the training data set can be modeled by the Closest Class Means tool.

Calculation

Consider data that give four measurements associated with each of three types of iris. If we have additional sets of measurements that we want to put into these classes, we can use the Closest Class Means tool.

Building the Model

The model is built using examples from the training data set.

Examples of values in the training set follow.

Measurement A	Measurement B	Measurement C	Measurement D	Class of iris
0.224	0.624	0.067	0.043	Setosa
0.11	0.502	0.051	0.043	Setosa
0.196	0.667	0.067	0.043	Setosa
0.055	0.584	0.067	0.082	Setosa
0.027	0.376	0.067	0.043	Setosa
0.749	0.502	0.627	0.541	Versicolor
0.722	0.459	0.663	0.584	Versicolor
0.612	0.333	0.612	0.584	Versicolor
0.557	0.541	0.612	0.498	Versicolor
0.639	0.376	0.627	0.624	Versicolor
0.557	0.416	0.831	0.831	Virginica
0.776	0.832	0.847	1	Virginica
0.612	0.416	0.812	0.875	Virginica
0.165	0.208	0.592	0.667	Virginica
0.667	0.208	0.812	0.71	Virginica

Training set examples

For each class, the class center is simply the mean of the four variables, as calculated from the training data set.

The means are shown below:

Measurement A	Measurement B	Measurement C	Measurement D	Class of iris
0.20692	0.622	0.07285	0.052	Setosa
0.52162	0.32715	0.58192	0.52231	Versicolor
0.64817	0.3785	0.79700	0.03342	Virginica

Class centers calculated from training data set

Using the Model

To classify, examples from the data set that is to be run (usually the test data set) are shown to the Closest Class Means tool. The Euclidean distance between the new example and each of the class centers is calculated.

Measurement A	Measurement B	Measurement C	Measurement D
0.667	0.459	0.627	0.584
0.557	0.584	0.78	0.957
0.027	0.416	0.051	0.043
0.361	0.416	0.525	0.498
0.471	0.416	0.643	0.71
0.196	0.624	0.051	0.082
0.333	0.251	0.576	0.459

Test data examples

To classify the first of the test records, we calculate its distance from class center 1, Setosa. This is calculated using the differences between the measurements for the test record and those of the Setosa center.

Its Euclidean distance from this center is:

$$\sqrt{(0.667 - 0.207)^2 + (0.459 - 0.622)^2 + (0.627 - 0.073)^2 + (0.584 - 0.052)^2} = 0.910$$

Distances from the other centers are computed in the same way. The distance to the Versicolor center is 0.211, and the distance to the Virginica center is 0.313. Since the distance is smallest to the Versicolor center, this example is assigned to the class Versicolor. Each of the records in the data set that is being run are then passed through the closest class means classifier and are assigned to a class.

Multiple Linear Regression

This section provides the following information:

- Outlines the multiple linear regression method
- Shows a sample calculation using the method

Method

Multiple linear regression is a classical statistical method that fits the examples to a straight line or plane.

The algorithm estimates the equation of the line or plane by finding that which gives the lowest error measure for the examples (the measure used is mean squared, although others could be used).

Calculation

Consider data containing two variables, x and y. There is a relationship between x and y, and the points for this distribution lie approximately on a straight line.

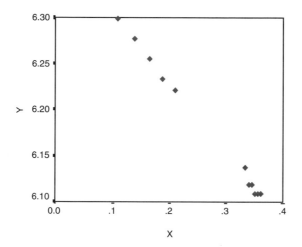

Building the Model

The model is built using examples from the training data set.

Examples of values in the training set are shown below:

Measurement X	Measurement Y
0.108508	6.2988
0.137698	6.2769
0.163968	6.2549
0.187611	6.2329
0.20889	6.2207
0.333625	6.1377
0.340302	6.1182
0.346312	6.1182
0.351721	6.1084
0.356589	6.1084
0.36097	6.1084

For two dimensions, the equation for a line is $y = mx + c$.

Multiple linear regression uses a least square fit to approximate the line. This minimizes the formula

$$\sum (y - \hat{y})^2$$

where y is the actual value and $\hat{y}$ is the value predicted by the line model.

This gives an equation for m,

$$m = \frac{\sum (x - \bar{x})(y - \bar{y})}{\sum (x - \bar{x})^2}$$

For this example:

$x = 0.272198$

$y = 6.174935$

$$\sum (x - \bar{x})(y - \bar{y}) = 0.08535$$

$$\sum (x - \bar{x})^2 = 0.113081$$

From this we can calculate m and c:

$m = -0.75478$

$c = y - mx = 6.380385$

This gives the estimated line $y = -0.75x + 6.38$, shown below.

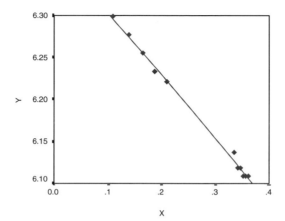

Using the Model

Once the parameters *m* and *c* have been calculated, values of *y* can be predicted by feeding the known value *x* into the equation for the line that we have calculated.

For example, if we wished to predict the value of *y* when *x* was 0.3:

$$y = (-0.75 \times 0.3) + 6.38$$

$$y = 6.155$$

Although this calculation has only used a two-dimensional example, the principal is readily extended to situations with more than two dimensions.

Principal Component Analysis

This section provides the following information:

- Outlines the principal component analysis method
- Shows a sample calculation using the method

Method

Principal component analysis is a well-established statistical method that reduces the number of fields required to represent the information in your data. This reduces the complexity of your data. Principal component analysis does not require output (target) fields, as these are not utilized during calculation.

The complexity of data is reduced by generating a set of axes, principal components, that are linear combinations of the input variables, and that account for the greatest possible variance of the input data. Principal components are ordered, so that the first principal component represents as much variance as possible, the second principal component, as much of the variance as was unaccounted for by the first principal component, and so on. The principal components are orthogonal to each other. The number of principal components desired can be specified, up to a maximum of the number of input fields in the data.

In practice the principal components of a data set are derived from the eigenvalues and eigenvectors of the correlation matrix, and it is the calculation of this matrix that forms the bulk of the calculation. The Principal Component Analysis tool uses an iterative method, Oja's technique, to determine the correlation matrix. Oja's technique is an iterative approach that is similar in many ways to the way in which a neural network learns but without a nonlinear element.

When the Principal Component Analysis tool is run, input records are mapped onto the set of axes that are the principal components.

Calculation

Consider data that give four measurements associated with each of three types of iris. If we want to reduce the number of input measurements from four to three we can use the Principal Component Analysis tool.

Building the Model

During training, the correlation matrix for the input variables of the training data set is calculated, and from this the eigenvalues and eigenvectors can be produced.

When presenting an input pattern X_p, composed of input elements x_0, x_1, x_2, ...x_{n-1}, to the Principal Component Analysis tool with n input fields, the parameters applied to each input element are given by a_i.

Algorithm

1. Set the values of the parameters to initial random values.

2. Show the network the input pattern X_p.

3. Calculate the output.

    The output is given by

    $$Z = \sum_{i=0}^{n-1} a_i \, x_i$$

4. Adjust the parameters.

    $$\Delta a_i (s+1) = \eta(x_i - Z a_i(s))$$

    where $a_i (s)$ is the parameter associated with input i at step s, Z is the output value, and η is a scaling coefficient.

5. Repeat actions 2 to 4 until a stable set of parameters a_i is reached.

Examples of values in the training set are shown below:

Measurement A (Input)	Measurement B (Input)	Measurement C (Input)	Measurement D (Input)	Class of iris (Output)
0.224	0.624	0.067	0.043	Setosa
0.11	0.502	0.051	0.043	Setosa
0.196	0.667	0.067	0.043	Setosa
0.055	0.584	0.067	0.082	Setosa
0.027	0.376	0.067	0.043	Setosa
0.749	0.502	0.627	0.541	Versicolor
0.722	0.459	0.663	0.584	Versicolor
0.612	0.333	0.612	0.584	Versicolor
0.557	0.541	0.612	0.498	Versicolor
0.639	0.376	0.627	0.624	Versicolor
0.557	0.416	0.831	0.831	Virginica
0.776	0.832	0.847	1	Virginica
0.612	0.416	0.812	0.875	Virginica
0.165	0.208	0.592	0.667	Virginica
0.667	0.208	0.812	0.71	Virginica

Training set examples

Note: *The Output field is not used by the Principal Component Analysis tool.*

The eigenvalues and eigenvectors for each principal component are given below:

		PCA_1	PCA_2	PCA_3
Eigenvalues:		2.95	0.78	0.239
Eigenvectors:				
	Measurement A	0.456	0.504	0.725
	Measurement B	-0.366	0.857	0.35
	Measurement C	0.586	0.0493	-0.285
	Measurement D	0.56	0.0985	-0.52

The eigenvalue for each principal component gives the proportion of the variance that is accounted for by that principal component.

The eigenvectors associated with each principal component give the coefficients that form the linear combination of the input variables used to generate that principal component.

Note: *Because Neural Connection automatically converts symbolic data into a 1-of-N encoding, each symbol in an input field is assigned its own set of eigenvectors by the Principal Component Analysis tool.*

Using the Model

When the Principal Component Analysis tool is run, input records are mapped onto the new fields defined by the principal components using the eigenvectors evaluated above. The mapping results in a data with new input fields but with the same output field (if relevant).

An example of the transformation follows.

No.	Measure A	Measure B	Measure C	Measure D	Class of iris
1	0.165	0.416	0.067	0.043	Setosa
2	0.584	0.502	0.592	0.584	Versicolor
3	0.416	0.29	0.694	0.749	Virginica
4	0.082	0.459	0.086	0.043	Setosa
5	0.333	0.125	0.51	0.498	Versicolor
6	0.557	0.376	0.78	0.71	Virginica
7	0.306	0.792	0.118	0.125	Setosa
8	0.388	0.333	0.592	0.498	Versicolor
9	0.918	0.416	0.949	0.831	Virginica
10	0.196	0.584	0.086	0.043	Setosa
11	0.165	0.169	0.388	0.376	Versicolor
12	0.835	0.376	0.898	0.71	Virginica
13	0.165	0.459	0.086	0.0	Setosa
14	0.251	0.29	0.49	0.541	Versicolor
15	0.804	0.667	0.863	1.0	Virginica

Untransformed data

No.	PCA 1	PCA 2	PCA 3	Class of iris
1	-0.2138	0.37383	-0.17928	Setosa
2	0.82257	0.87913	-0.20741	Versicolor
3	1.04462	0.46733	-0.20525	Virginica
4	-0.29874	0.37929	-0.23645	Setosa
5	0.79582	0.13041	-0.18817	Versicolor
6	1.12938	0.69564	-0.24302	Virginica
7	-0.3003	1.04072	-0.24779	Setosa
8	0.74033	0.48139	-0.23429	Versicolor
9	1.5572	1.03242	-0.12907	Virginica
10	-0.30562	0.64528	-0.21624	Setosa
11	0.45141	0.05764	-0.2369	Versicolor
12	1.44123	0.89982	-0.12113	Virginica
13	-0.26186	0.43425	-0.1841	Setosa
14	0.6156	0.31905	-0.28585	Versicolor
15	1.359	1.33411	-0.28983	Virginica

Transformed data

Multi-Layer Perceptron

This section provides the following information:

- Outlines the Multi-Layer Perceptron method
- Gives the algorithm used to train Multi-Layer Perceptrons
- Explains how trained Multi-Layer Perceptrons are used

Method

The Multi-Layer Perceptron is a supervised neural network that learns the mapping between input data and target data.

The Multi-Layer Perceptron is built from a series of connected processing elements or neurons. These are grouped in layers, and have connections to preceding and following layers, but not to other neurons within the layer. Neurons in the input layer each receive an input from the data—typically each neuron represents one field in the input data. Neurons in the output layer provide outputs to the system— typically each output neuron represents one target field in the problem.

The Multi-Layer Perceptron is based on the original Simple Perceptron model but with additional layers of neurons between the input and output layers.

Simple Perceptrons

A Simple Perceptron consists of an input layer and an output layer of neurons. Each processing element in the input layer is connected to each processing element in the output layer, and these connections have weights associated with them. These weights are adjusted as the network is trained. The inputs to any processing element in a Perceptron are a product of the input data and the associated connection weightings.

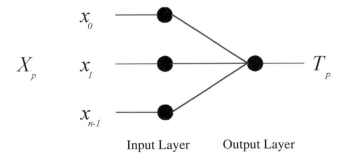

The output from a processing element is the input modified by an activation, or transfer function. In the case of the Simple Perceptron, the transfer function was usually linear, a simple summation.

Given any input pattern, a Perceptron gives a set of output values from the neurons in the output layer that depends on the input pattern and on the values of the connections.

Multi-Layer Perceptrons

Multi-Layer Perceptrons differ from Simple Perceptrons in that they have one or more additional layers of neurons, known as hidden layers, that lie between the input and output layers. The functionality of hidden and output layer neurons is the same as in the case of simple Perceptrons, while the transfer function is a smooth nonlinear function, usually the sigmoid function. This function is chosen because the algorithm requires a response function with a continuous, single-valued first derivative.

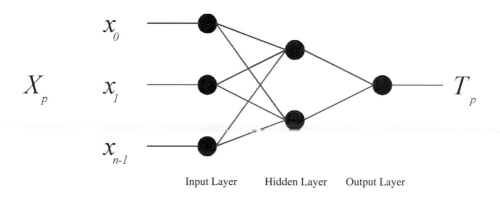

Input Layer   Hidden Layer   Output Layer

Training proceeds in the following way. First, the weights and biases in the network are initialized, usually to small random values. A training pattern is then applied to the input units and the activations of neurons in the first hidden layer are calculated. The outputs produced by these neurons via the transfer function are then fed on to neurons in the following layer. This forward pass process is repeated at each layer until an output signal from neurons in the output layer is obtained.

The difference between the actual and desired output values is measured, and the network model connection strengths are changed so that the outputs produced by the network become closer to the desired outputs. This is achieved by a backward pass during which connection changes are propagated back through the network starting with the connections to the output layer and ending with those to the input layer.

The basic method for adapting the connections, the learning rule, is simple. If the output produced by the network is correct, the connections from the output neurons to all input neurons are unchanged. If the networks output is larger than the desired output at any node, then the connections between that neuron and all input neurons are decreased. If the outputs are smaller than desired, the connection values are increased.

Calculation

The calculation associated with a Multi-Layer Perceptron can be split into two parts: building the model, and using the model.

The actual calculations undertaken during building and using models are complex and are extremely dependent on the problem being modeled and the data being used. Rather than looking at a specific example, the calculation shown here looks at the algorithm used during model building and how this is reflected in using the model.

Building the Model

Building the model, more commonly known as the training process, takes place in the following way.

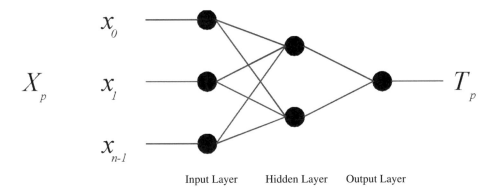

When presenting an input pattern X_p, composed of input elements x_0, x_1, x_2, ...x_{n-1}, that is related to a target pattern T_p to a Multi-Layer Perceptron with n input nodes. The weights between nodes i and j in the Multi-Layer Perceptron are given by w_{ij}.

Training Algorithm

1. Set the values of the weights to initial random values.

2. Show the network the input pattern X_p and the target pattern T_p.

3. Calculate the output from each node in a layer.

    The output from a node j in the second layer is given by

    $$z_j = \phi \sum_{i=0}^{n-1} w_{ij} x_i$$

    where ϕ is the activation, or transfer function, of the node.

4. Adjust the weights between nodes, starting from the output layer and working backwards.

    $$w_{ij}(s+1) = w_{ij}(s) + \eta \delta_{pj} z_{pj}$$

    where $w_{ij}(s)$ is the weight between nodes i and j at step s, z_{pj} is output value at node j, and δ_{pj} is the error of pattern p at node j and η is the activation function.

5. Repeat actions 2 to 4 until the error between the target and output reaches a global minimum.

If this algorithm is used simply as stated, there is a significant chance that overtraining will take place. Overtraining is said to have occurred when a model learns the training data too precisely and loses the ability to generalize solutions for the problem. To prevent this from occurring, the data used during training are split into two data sets, the training data set and the validation data set.

The training data set is used in the algorithm shown above and is the data which the neural network uses to learn the solution to the problem. The validation data set is used to establish when to stop the algorithm; that is, to choose the best solution. To do this, after every training iteration the validation data set is passed through the network, and the error over the data set is calculated. The best set of weights are defined as those that produce the lowest error over the validation data set.

Using the Model

Once the best solution has been found, the weights are fixed, and no further training takes place.

To generate a new output, an input pattern is shown to the inputs. The output is then generated at the output layer.

Radial Basis Function

This section provides the following information:

- Outlines the Radial Basis Function method

- Gives the algorithm used to train Radial Basis Functions

- Explains how trained Radial Basis Functions are used

Method

The Radial Basis Function is a supervised neural network that learns the mapping between input data and target data.

Radial basis functions build classifications from ellipses and hyperellipses that partition the input data space. These hyperellipses are defined by radial functions (ϕ) of the type

$$\phi(\| x - y \|)$$

where $\|...\|$ is a distance measure between an input pattern x and a center y that is positioned in the input data space. These centers are defined by the weights associated with the inputs to the nodes in the hidden layer of the Radial Basis Function.

The function f in k dimensional space that partitions the space is composed of elements f_k, where

$$f_k = \sum_{j=1}^{m} \lambda_{jk} \phi(\|x - y_j\|)$$

This linear combination requires only the solution of the linear coefficients λ_{jk}.

Calculation

The calculation associated with a Radial Basis Function can be split into two parts: building the model, and using the model.

The actual calculations undertaken during building and using models are complex and are extremely dependent on the problem being modeled and the data being used. Rather than looking at a specific example, the calculation shown here looks at the algorithm that is used during model building and how this is reflected in using the model.

Building the Model

Since this problem can be solved exactly using linear optimization techniques, a best fit can be found that relies only on the number and positions of the centers, and on the choice of nonlinear function used. Unlike the case of the Multi-Layer Perceptron, the weights to the nodes in the hidden layer are not changed during training.

Training Algorithm

1. Select the desired number of centers.

2. Select the values of the weights that "position" the centers.

3. Calculate the values $\phi(\| x{-}y \|)$ of all the input patterns for all the centers.

4. Solve the linear equations

$$f_k = \sum_{j=1}^{m} \lambda_{jk} \phi(\| x - y_j \|)$$

Note: In Neural Connection, this equation is solved using the multiple linear regression technique.

In practice it is difficult to establish the correct number of centers and their optimal positioning before training starts. In order to circumvent this problem, a number of options are available, including different center placement strategies and increasing the number of centers incrementally.

Using the Model

Once the solution for the linear equation has been found, the value of the output for any input can be calculated using the equations

$$f_k = \sum_{j-1}^{m} \lambda_{jk} \phi(\| x - y_j \|)$$

Bayesian Network

This section provides the following information:

- Outlines the Bayesian method
- Gives the algorithm used to train Bayesian Networks
- Explains how trained Bayesian Networks are used

Method

Bayesian statistics concentrate on how probabilities are affected by prior knowledge, and by posterior knowledge—that is, by what we know about a situation before and after we examine the data.

Bayes' rule states that the probability of the network being in a state w, given that an event D has occurred, is equal to the likelihood that the event D would occur if the network was in state w, multiplied by the probability of the network being in the state w regardless of any events, divided by the probability of the event D occurring, regardless of the state of the network:

$$P(w|D) = \frac{P(D|w) \cdot P(w)}{P(D)}$$

Rather than using a new neural network architecture, Bayesian statistics allow us to apply this probabilistic approach to an existing type of network. The Bayesian Network is the application of Bayesian statistics to the Multi-Layer Perceptron, and as such has many features in common with that neural network. The major difference is in the way that the error measure, or accuracy of the network, is calculated.

In conventional Multi-Layer Perceptrons, the learning rule changes the weights on connections to minimize an error measure. This error measure is usually measured using the generalized delta rule, where the error over a data set D is given by:

$$E_D = \sum_x E_x = \frac{1}{2} \sum_x \sum_j (t_{xj} - a_{xj})^2$$

Where

x is an example from the training set

j is an output from the mode

t_{xj} is a target value

a_{xj} is the network output

By contrast, Bayesian Networks are trained to minimize a cost function C, where

$$C = \beta E_D + \alpha E_W$$

where E_W is a weight penalizing function.

The weight penalizing function is included on the assumption that the underlying function that creates the training set is smoother than that function and the noise in the data set.

α and β are known as *hyperparameters*. When Bayesian networks train, a goal is to determine appropriate levels for these parameters. Both α and β are coefficients that are related to the noise of the data set, a value that will almost certainly be unknown, and are linked by the equation

$$\alpha - \xi\beta$$

However, as training is intended to minimize the cost function, it is only necessary to find the correct ratio of α and β, that is, the weight decay factor ξ.

Within a network the adjustable parameters can be said to exist in natural groups. So, for example, the weights between the input layer and hidden layer of a Multi-Layer Perceptron could be said to be a group. The exact definition and number of such groups remain a choice for the network designer. The Bayesian Network tool assigns separate weight decay factors to each parameter group, such that for every group, g

$$\alpha_g = \xi_g \beta$$

This enables us to redefine the cost function as

$$C = E_D + \sum_g \xi_g E_{Wg}$$

It can be shown that we can calculate error measures for ξ_g during training, and that assuming a Gaussian noise distribution

$$\sigma_{\log \xi_g} = \sqrt{\frac{2}{\gamma_g}}$$

where:

γ_g is the number of parameters in group g that are *well-determined* by the training data set.

A well-determined parameter is one that has been derived from the training data, rather than from the probability density function of the variable.

Calculation

As with MLP training, the Bayesian Network repeatedly applies error back-propagation to minimize the cost function of the network. However, unlike the MLP, the Bayesian Network also dynamically adjusts the values of the hyperparameters. These values are adjusted to enable the hyperparameters to fit the noise in the training data set.

During training, the Bayesian Network assumes that the inputs and outputs are taken from a prior Gaussian distribution. In order to better fit this assumption, all inputs and outputs are normalized using *zero mean standard deviation* normalization.

Training Algorithm

1. Initialize adjustable parameters with random values from a Gaussian distribution.

2. Set the initial weight decay parameters, by recording the error, E, on an initial pass of the data.

$$\xi_g = \frac{E^2}{4}$$

3. Show the network the input pattern X_p and the target pattern T_p.

4. Calculate the output from each node in a layer for every input and target pattern.

5. Adjust the weight decay parameters, and recalculate the number of well-determined parameters.

6. Repeat steps 3 to 5 until the network stabilizes.

Using the Model

Once the best solution has been found, the weights are fixed, and no further training takes place.

To generate a new output, an input pattern is shown to the inputs. The output is then generated at the output layer.

Kohonen Network

This section provides the following information:

* Outlines the Kohonen Network method

* Gives the algorithm used to train Kohonen networks

* Explains how trained Kohonen networks are used

Method

The Kohonen Network is an unsupervised neural network that produces a self-organized map of the data presented to it during training. Kohonen networks group input data based on common features in the data. There is no concept of target data associated with a Kohonen network. One advantage of the Kohonen Network is that it does not make assumptions about the number of different groups, or clusters, that are present within the data.

Structure

Kohonen networks are constructed from a layer of nodes, each of which is connected to all the input fields. This layer is known as the Kohonen layer.

The connections between the nodes and the inputs have an associated weight. Unlike the Multi-Layer Perceptron or the Radial Basis Function, there is no output layer. The outputs produced are derived from the outputs of the nodes in the Kohonen layer.

Calculation

The calculation associated with a Kohonen network can be split into two parts, building the model, and using the model.

The actual calculations undertaken during building and using models are complex and are extremely dependent on the problem being modeled and the data being used. Rather than looking at a specific example, the calculation shown here looks at the algorithm that is used during model building and how this is reflected in using the model.

Building the Model

When presenting an input pattern X_p, composed of input elements x_0, x_1, x_2, ...x_{n-1}, to a Kohonen network with n input nodes, the weight between an input i and a node j is given by w_{ij}.

Training Algorithm

1. Initialize the weights between inputs and the nodes.

2. Present an input x_0, x_1, x_2, ...x_{n-1}.

3. Calculate the error measurement between the input and the weights, in this case using the Euclidean distance

$$d_j = \sum_{i=0}^{n-1} (x_i - w_{ij})^2$$

4. Select the node $j*$ that has the minimum value of d_j.

5. Update the weights for node $j*$ and its neighbors to be

$$w_{ij}* = w_{ij} + \eta(x_i - w_{ij})$$

where η is the learning rate of the Kohonen layer, and typically decays over time. The neighborhood size is defined before the model is built, and again typically decays over time.

6. Repeat steps 2 to 4 until the weights have stabilized.

Using the Model

Once the model has been built, a new input pattern X_p can be shown to the Kohonen network, and various outputs can be produced.

Full Response

The output is given as the outputs d_j of every node in the Kohonen layer.

Vector Quantization

The output is given as the set of weights w_{ij} of the winning node $j*$ that has the minimum value of d_j.

Vector Quantization Codebook

Each node in the Kohonen layer is given a code number. The output is the code of the winning node $j*$ that has the minimum value of d_j.

General Reference

Appendix IV

Neural Networks

The human brain is the most powerful computer that exists. It routinely carries out tasks which the biggest silicon supercomputer would not begin to cope with, so it would seem sensible to try to model the way a computer works on the way a brain works. This, however, leads to problems. We all think (with varying degrees of success), but *how* do we think? How do we recognize the face of a friend? How do we learn? How do we make decisions? How do we remember things? Answering these questions becomes vital if any progress is to be made towards producing a brain-like computer.

Fortunately, physiological and psychological research has given us some understanding of many of the brain's mechanisms, including the powers of association, generalization, and self-organization. But each of these principles requires the simultaneous action of many separate neural processing units towards a common goal, and this simultaneity causes problems when we try to reproduce it using conventional serial computers.

Unlike conventional computers, the brain does not have a single central processing unit connected to a memory store. Instead, it distributes its processing tasks among millions of simple nerve cells called *neurons*. It routinely handles communications among millions of cells, each of which is constantly sending and receiving information.

Neurons

Neurons are the fundamental building blocks of an animal or human nervous system. Each neuron is a single cell, which receives signals from other cells through input structures called *dendrites*. These signals are then combined within the cell body of the neuron, and if the combined strength of these signals reaches a certain value the neuron fires and sends a signal to its output, the *axon*. Within a neuron, these signals take the form of electrical pulses, and a strong signal causes pulses to happen more frequently.

While the signals within a neuron are electrical, those between neurons are chemical. The axon from each cell connects to the dendrites of many other cells, through junctions called *synapses*. Transmission across these junctions takes place through the action of chemicals called *neurotransmitters*. Neurotransmitters are produced only when the electrical pulses on the axon reach the synapse. The signal strength now depends upon the amount of chemical released by the axon and received by the dendrite of the next cell.

In 1949, Donald Hebb, in his book *The Organization of Behavior* suggested that the behavior of these synapses was modified by learning. He proposed that an increase in the electrical activity at a synapse would increase the capacity of the synapse to produce neurotransmitters. The experiences of the external world would cause neural activity, which would strengthen the connections between stimulated neurons, and this would result in the brain learning. Learning would therefore leave some synapses enhanced, while others would remain dormant.

Thus we have a picture of a brain as a highly interconnected network of neurons, with connections whose effectiveness varies as a result of an organism's sensory experience. It is this idea that forms the basis of artificial neural computers.

Artificial Neural Networks

Neural computing (or neural network computing) seeks to use these principles, creating a simplified model of the brain by using a network of artificial neurons. At present, most of these models are software simulations that work on serial computers, although some are implemented in silicon, or by using optical techniques.

In an artificial neural network, the unit that performs the task of a biological neuron is known as a *processing element*, *node*, or *neuron*. A processing element (PE) has a number of inputs (analogous to the dendrites in a biological neural network), that it combines, usually by means of a simple summation, to form an internal activation level.

In a biological neuron, the cell fires and produces an output only if the activity level within the cell reaches a certain threshold value. In a similar way, the internal activation level of a processing element is modified by means of a transfer function, before being sent as an output signal to another neuron in the network. This transfer function can be a simple step threshold function, which passes information only if the activity level reaches a certain value, or a continuous function of the processing element' s activity.

The output of a processing element is connected to the inputs of other processing elements. Each connection has a weight, or scaling factor, associated with it. This is the analogue of a synaptic strength in a biological network.

The signals that arrive at the inputs to a processing element are modified by these weights before being summed. This means that the internal activation level is, in fact, a weighted sum of the inputs. As with a biological system, the values of these connection weights change in response to information entering the network. This gives the network the ability to learn.

Why Should We Use Neural Networks?

Conventional computing has produced good solutions to many problems, so why should you change your techniques now? What advantages can Neural Networks give you over tried and tested conventional computing?

With the enormous developments in computer hardware over the last thirty years, the factors that limit the use of computers are no longer speed and program size restrictions; the computer on your desk has more raw power than large mainframes did a decade ago. The central problem that limits computers today is the difficulty of producing software. Programs have become difficult and expensive to produce and maintain, even in those areas where the algorithms—the recipe of steps that become the program when coded into a computing language—are known. For many problems, such as speech recognition, there is a more fundamental problem: no really good algorithms are known. We do not know how we are able to recognize a face in a crowd and therefore cannot write down the sequence of steps necessary to tell a computer how to do so.

Our own most personal computers, our brains, manage to do most of their tasks without being programmed explicitly. Many of the complex tasks that people do with ease are learned by example.

Wouldn't it be nice if we could treat a computer as an information processing black box, and train it just by giving it some examples? Neural networks are an attempt to do just that.

Serial Computers

Any computing system can be thought of as a black box. The box is designed to perform some specified task; it receives information as input, processes that information, and then produces some output results. If you think of computers in this way, then all computers are conceptually the same; they differ only in terms of what goes on inside the black box.

A conventional computer, such as the one on your desk, has two components inside the box: the hardware and the software. It has a single large processing unit, the CPU, connected to some memory. It also has mechanisms for communicating with the outside world via a keyboard, display screen, and so on.

The software on a computer consists of a series of instructions, with data. Instructions are executed one at a time, sequentially. A computer that processes instructions in this way is called a *serial* computer. When you write software for such a computer, you have to break down the problem into a series of steps to match the serial processing.

To increase the power of your computer, you may have special processing units that take care of the display or of reading and writing to disk. Although the black box may now contain a number of processors, there is still one main processor that runs through its programs one step at a time. For problems that must process very large amounts of data, then you could use an even more powerful computer called a *parallel processor*.

Any problem that is computable can be programmed on a serial computer and the steps in the computation carried out sequentially. This is relatively slow because only one thing is being done at a time. Electronic computers are able to use this method of computation and produce results in an acceptable time only because they are fast.

In contrast, brains are made of building blocks that process signals much more slowly. Although brains do some high level reasoning tasks sequentially, most of the computationally demanding tasks, such as vision, must be done using parallel processing.

The basic response time of a neuron (a biological nerve cell) is measured in milliseconds. Using very large numbers of neurons, people are able to recognize objects in front of their eyes in perhaps a tenth of a second. These facts together mean that if our brains were recognizing visual patterns using a serial program, then that program would have only a few hundred steps at most. Despite many years of research in computer vision, nobody knows how to write such a program.

Parallel Computers

In a parallel computer, there are a number of processing units, each of which can run a copy of the software, or different software, simultaneously. These processors are organized so that they can share the information coming into the black box, with each processor working on one part of it. Organizing a computer to work in this way is a very complex task, and the task becomes even worse if one processor must wait until another finishes before it can start. As a result, parallel computers are expensive and more difficult to program than serial computers.

Even with this degree of complexity, no commercial parallel computer can match the power of the human brain in its ability to think, to remember, and to reason. The apparent ease with which the brain can learn to understand speech or recognize faces in a crowd has led one group of researchers to seek ways of building computers that act more like the brain; in particular, machines that can be trained by example. Their efforts have led to the development of neural network computing.

Feed-Forward and Feedback Networks

A neural network consists of many processing elements, or neurons, joined together with weighted connections. There are two main types of neural network: feed-forward networks and feedback networks.

In a feed-forward network, no neuron's output is directly dependent on any of its previous output values. Information flows in one direction only—from input to output. There are no feedback loops within the system. Once trained, feed-forward networks always give the same response for the same input.

The most important class of feed-forward networks is the Multi-Layer Perceptron or MLP. This actually refers to a large family of networks with the common factor that they are trained by propagating errors back through the network. For this reason, they are often called *back propagation* or *backprop nets*.

In a feedback network, the output of a neuron may be connected, via some path, back to its input. The outputs of neurons in a feedback network are always dependent on the previous state of the network. Such networks do not necessarily give the correct answer as soon as a new data value is presented to the network. Instead, the data circulates within the network as it converges to a solution. As there is usually some random element present either in the data or in the initial state of the network, a feedback network does not always converge to exactly the same solution for a given input.

There are a number of different neural network models that use feedback, including some variations of backprop nets called *recurrent* networks. The Hopfield network, which started most of the current activity in neural network computing, is also in this category.

Layers of Neurons

In the most important neural network models, groups of neurons are arranged in groups or layers. Feed-forward networks usually have several layers. Each layer gets its input from the preceding layer while its output forms the input to the succeeding layer. Feedback networks are more complex, with some models having connections among the neurons within a layer.

The input layer receives input from the outside world. In a feed-forward network, this is the only way in which the input layer can receive information. There are no interconnections among these input neurons. The output from the input layer neurons forms the input to the first hidden layer.

The output layer of neurons receives its input from the hidden layer and sends its output signal to the outside world. It is this layer that provides the network's decision or prediction for any given input.

Between the input and output layers, there are one or more *hidden* layers. A hidden layer is composed of neurons which are connected to neurons in other layers but not to the outside world. It is the presence of these hidden layers that give the network the ability to provide solutions to many real world problems.

A hidden layer is used by the network to create an internal representation of the problem. In effect, it recodes the input into a form that captures the features in the training data set.

By recoding the data in terms of these features, the network can generalize from the training data set to provide the most appropriate output for new or noisy data.

One or more neurons in the hidden layer recode each specific feature in the input data. The coding is represented by the weights between the input layer and the hidden layer. When a new data value is presented to the input of the network, the strengths of the outputs from the neurons in the hidden layer represent a component of each feature. These outputs are decoded by the weights from the hidden to output layer in order to form a meaningful output.

Numbers of Neurons and Layers

The number of neurons in the input and output layers is initially determined by the number of input and output data values. In the simplest case, there is one neuron in the input layer for each data attribute. For a decision network, there is one output for each decision class. (In the case of a simple yes/no decision, although there are two classes, the problem can be represented by a single output neuron). For a prediction network, there is one output neuron for each predicted value.

The number of hidden layers and the number of neurons to use in each layer are determined by the number of features in the training data and the relationships between them. It can be shown mathematically that any problem can be represented by using, at most, two hidden layers of neurons with nonlinear transfer functions.

Neural Networks and Other Approaches

Neural networks may sound strange at first, but they have clear relationships to two other major areas of computing: expert systems and statistical pattern recognition methods. A full description of these methods and the links to neural computing would take too long to discuss here, but the next two sections sketch the outlines.

Neural Networks and Expert Systems

Expert systems are computer programs meant to mimic the thought processes used by a human expert. They are used in areas such as medical diagnosis or configuring computer systems—problems that people solve by conscious, goal directed reasoning. They are usually written by the laborious process of trying to find out what an expert does and then writing down his or her knowledge as a set of rules in the computer program, or expert system.

In an expert system, the methods for processing the incoming information are separated from the information itself. This allows software developers to spend a lot of time and effort producing a single, general purpose program that will process information in many different ways and be useful for a wide range of tasks. This program is termed an *expert system shell*.

You can make this general shell work on your specific information by giving the shell specific rules on how the information should be processed. You can find these rules by talking to experts within your organization and asking them how they would perform the task.

Consider the problem of writing a computer program for medical diagnosis, a field for which many prototype expert systems have been built. The process would be to try to find out how a doctor thinks and what rules he or she uses to make a diagnosis, and then to code those rules explicitly in a computer program.

There is another approach. Suppose you had access to a large set of case histories—that is, collections of symptoms observed in the patients, together with the doctor's diagnoses. These symptoms are attributes that could be coded onto a neural network. Similarly, the diagnoses, the doctor's decisions, could provide the output layer in a network. You could then use a neural network to learn to associate diagnoses with sets of symptoms from the training data set of case histories. Prototype systems have been built for some areas of medical diagnosis, and their performance level is similar to that of specialist clinicians.

Neural Networks and Pattern Recognition

Humans are very good at pattern recognition—tasks such as identifying a face or reading a signature. These tasks require the ability to match large amounts of input data with some representation of the data, such as the name of the person in a photograph. Think, for example, of the number of people you know and how quickly you can identify them.

Pattern recognition systems must not deal with large amounts of data only; they must also deal with noisy or incomplete data. For example, you can still recognize the faces of people you know even if they have changed their hairstyles.

Neural networks are trained to find patterns in a set of training data. They are therefore clearly pattern recognizers, and have much in common with other statistical pattern recognition techniques. Neural networks, with their ability to generalize and to learn by example, make good pattern recognition systems. Generalization, achieved by selecting combinations of internal features to represent the problem, gives them some advantages over the more common statistical techniques; while the ability to learn and adapt to new data gives them an edge over expert systems for many tasks.

The relationship between neural networks and particular statistical pattern recognition methods is now well established.

Neural Connection uses several conventional pattern recognition techniques, which are described below.

Closest Class Mean Classifier

The Closest Class Mean (CCM) algorithm is a simple classifier that is easy to compute, and that gives good results if the data examples are well clustered.

During the training phase, the CCM classifier computes a vector mean for each of the decision classes. Each vector mean consists of a mean value for each of the data attributes. In effect, the CCM classifier produces a typical example of each of the decision classes.

At run time, the distances between the new, unknown, data vector and each of the class mean vectors are measured. The new vector is assigned to the class with the smallest distance.

Although a CCM classifier is fast, it gives poor results if the training data examples contain a significant number of outliers. These tend to bias the class means in the direction of the outliers and this leads to poorer classification performance.

Regression Analysis

For problems which involve prediction, the most widely used statistical technique is regression analysis. Given a training set of noisy data, regression analysis tries to find a functional relationship between the input variables or attributes and the output. Once this relationship is found, then a predicted output for a new set of input variables, not in the original training set, can be computed.

Statistical regression methods make two critical assumptions. The first is that the inputs and the output are linearly related. The second is that there is no interaction among the input variables. Neural networks can outperform regression analysis because they are capable of representing nonlinear relationships, and they can deal with the correlations between variables.

There is another important difference between the two approaches. If you are using statistical techniques, then you specify the model to be used before computations can be performed. Often these models are based on simplifying assumptions about the underlying distribution of data. If the model performs well, as judged by testing against unseen validation data, then the model can be used to provide an interpretation of the data.

Neural networks, on the other hand, generate their own underlying models of the data. Networks are thus more robust (able to predict more accurately over a wider range of input data) when the underlying processes are nonlinear and the statistics non-Gaussian. Networks can also adapt their models in response to new data. The disadvantage is that the underlying model may be difficult or even impossible to extract from the network, leaving you uncertain as to why the network made a particular prediction.

Learning by Example

Conventional computers have their information and instructions embedded in a single program. In expert systems, knowledge is made explicit in the form of rules. Neural networks generate their own rules by being shown examples of a problem. They learn about a problem by using a learning rule to change the connection weights of the network in response to example inputs and, optionally, desired outputs.

There are two main kinds of learning used by neural network models: supervised learning and unsupervised learning.

Supervised Learning

The term *supervised learning* comes from the idea of a teacher whose function is to correct the network's response to a set of inputs. The training data consist of a number of examples, each of which has a set of input values together with an associated desired output. Each set of inputs is presented to the network, which then produces an output. This output is then compared with the correct output for the current set of inputs. The "teacher" then causes the network to change its internal representation of the data in a principled way so as to capture the essential features of the input data.

In the algorithm, the teacher is actually the learning rule that specifies how the weights are to be updated.

This form of learning is well understood and has been used in the majority of successful neural network applications.

Unsupervised Learning

In unsupervised leaning, there is no teacher involved. Instead, the network is presented with the set of training inputs, and it creates its own representation of the input data. This self-organizing behavior may involve competition, cooperation, or both.

For all methods of unsupervised learning, neurons are organized into groups, or layers. For competitive learning, the neurons in each group are connected together so that if one neuron gives a high level of output, it tends to inhibit the outputs of the other neurons. Thus, the neurons in each group compete with each other for the right to represent a particular feature. Once a particular neuron in the group begins to respond more strongly to a particular input, it suppresses its neighbors and thus wins the competition.

Eventually, each cluster of neurons comes to represent different features in the data.

In cooperative learning, the neurons within each cluster work together to reinforce their outputs. This process usually involves some form of feedback together with a decay process. If too few of the neurons in a group respond to an input, then the activity of the group as a whole is too small to contribute to the network activity. If a sufficient number of neurons respond, then the feedback reinforces the activity, ensuring that the group as a whole becomes responsive to the particular input.

Unsupervised learning has so far made less impact in practical neural network applications than supervised methods.

Distributed Associative Memory

Conventional computers store a single piece of information in a single memory location. In a neural network, memory is distributed over the connection weights. These weights form an internal representation of the problem on which the network was trained. A single fact is represented by many weights. In turn, each weight contributes to the memory of many different weights.

Some types of neural network have another property of memory, called *association*. An associative network is one in which information can be recalled when only a partial input is present. The network chooses the closest match in memory to the partial input, and generates an output that corresponds to a stored input.

This property of association allows the network to generate a reasonable response, even when presented with incomplete, noisy, or previously unseen input.

Fault Tolerance

The distributed nature of information storage in a neural network provides another advantage that has not yet been widely exploited. Since conventional computers store a single piece of information in a single memory location, they can fail completely if even a small amount of memory is damaged.

Neural networks store information in a distributed way across the connection strengths of the entire network. If some processing elements fail or their connections' strengths are altered slightly, then the behavior of the network as a whole is only slightly degraded. As more processing elements fail, then the performance of the network is degraded a little more. The performance of a neural network therefore degrades slowly and not catastrophically as faults occur. The full advantage of this property will not be evident until neural networks are implemented directly in hardware.

Such a system is called *fault tolerant*. Performance suffers as faults occur, but the system as a whole does not come to an abrupt halt. Of course, if the neural network is simulated on a conventional computer, then it fails in just the same way as a spreadsheet program if the central processor fails. But if the network is implemented optically or by using multiple VLSI processors, then this fault tolerance becomes an important factor. Networks will become increasingly important for such tasks as plant operation, missile guidance, or the control of remote space craft, where catastrophic failure could bring disaster.

Decisions and Predictions

There are two ways of representing problems with neural networks: decision networks and prediction networks.

A decision network takes an input and tries to associate it with one of a number of previously defined output categories. It decides which is the most appropriate output for the particular input—for example, a credit assessment network that gives a *yes* or *no* response to an application.

A prediction network gives a single value representative of the input. For example, the inputs may represent the operations involved in the machining of mechanical components, while the output represents the manufacturing cost. The network is trained on example components, each of which has an associated cost. Given a new component, the network interpolates between its training examples to predict the cost of the new part.

A Brief History of Neural Networks

Birth of Neural Networks

Most people who start to work with neural networks are surprised to find that neural networks are not new but have a history as long as more conventional methods of computing. In part, this is due to the links with biology. It was in the 1790s that Luigi Galvani, an Italian, first made the connection between electricity and the nervous system, with his experiments on frog legs. Real neurons have been observed since at least the last century, and by the end of the nineteenth century, histologists and anatomists had established the presence of neurons and had shown how axons and dendrites were interconnected in complex networks.

The first mathematical attempt to explain what a network of neurons could calculate came in a paper in 1943, by neurobiologist Warren McCulloch and statistician Walter Pitts. They showed that a network composed of binary-valued neurons was capable of performing computations. In 1949, Donald Hebb, in his book *Organization of Behavior* proposed a method by which learning could take place in networks. These ideas formed the basis of the new science of neural computing.

During the 1950s, the dominant researchers in the field of neural computing were Frank Rosenblatt and Bernard Widrow. Rosenblatt invented a pattern classification network which could identify simple shapes, based on a processing element called a *perceptron*. The perceptron was capable of some learning and limited generalization, allowing it to correctly categorize some classes of patterns, even when there was noise on its inputs. Widrow invented a somewhat similar technique, named Adaline (**Ada**ptive **Lin**ear **E**lement), which had a more sophisticated learning algorithm.

Although Rosenblatt's perceptron spurred research in neural computing during the 60s, it had many limitations. Most importantly, it was a linear device and could not solve problems that involved nonlinear relationships among inputs and outputs. This and other seemingly insurmountable limitations were pointed out by Marvin Minsky and Seymour Papert in their book, *Perceptrons*, published in 1969.

The Dark Ages

The influence that *Perceptrons* had on the computing community was so great that virtually all sources of funding for neural computing research dried up. It effectively condemned neural networks as a dead end for computing and resulted in a switch to research into expert systems. Yet, despite the influence of the book, a few researchers continued their work.

James Anderson, of Brown University, concentrated on the development of linear associative memory models, based on Hebbian learning principles. He extended this work to produce a network called *brain-state-in-a-box*.

Teuvo Kohonen, of the Helsinki Technical University, built on earlier work by David Willshaw and von der Malsberg, and developed competitive learning algorithms that preserve topographic mappings in the pattern space.

Kohonen's models came to be of particular interest to biologists wishing to model the topographic mappings that occur in human senses.

Stephen Grossberg, of Boston University, was another researcher interested in the neurobiological aspects of neural networks. Based on this research, he developed a class of networks that use Adaptive Resonance Theory. These networks use single pass learning and are self-organizing, requiring no teacher during the training phase.

Rebirth of Neural Computing

In 1982, John Hopfield, of the California Institute of Technology, published a paper in the *Proceedings of the National Academy of Sciences.* It was the first time since the publication of *Perceptrons* in the 1960s that a paper on neural computing had been published by the Academy. The paper described a novel memory model and showed how its properties could be analyzed using methods familiar to statistical physicists. Hopfield's key ideas were the addition of nonlinearities to the system and the concept of describing the state of a network in terms of a global energy function. Solutions to a problem were *minima* in this global energy function: the lower the *minima,* the better the solution.

These developments at last overcame the problems that perceptrons had come up against and, coupled with Hopfield's personal standing, stimulated a wave of neural network research.

The most significant neural network architecture developed since the resurgence of interest in the subject is the multi-layer perceptron, also referred to as a *back propagation network* after the learning rule it uses.

Barely a research conference goes by without someone claiming that he actually invented this idea earlier, but Rumelhart, Hinton, and Williams must take the credit for the practical impact, since it was their paper that has stimulated the enormous wave of research and practical application that has followed.

Glossary

1-of-N encoding
A way of encoding symbolic variables that removes the danger of implying false linear relationships between categories.

activation function
An element of a neuron in a Multi-Layer Perceptron. A smooth nonlinear function that is used to modify the summed inputs to the neuron.

back propagation
An aspect of the learning algorithm used in a Multi-Layer Perceptron. It refers to using the error generated at the output layer of neurons to alter the weights between neurons in previous layers. Multi-Layer Perceptrons are sometimes referred to as back propagation networks.

centers
A name used for the neurons in a Radial Basis Function. Each neuron can be thought of as being located at a position in the input data space and as being the center of a radial function.

classification problem
A problem that places an example into one of a discreet number of categories.

clipping
A preprocessing technique that replaces extreme data points with more appropriate values. Sometimes known as *trimming*.

Closest Class Mean
A linear statistical method for classifying an example into one of a discreet number of categories.

conjugate gradient
A learning algorithm that is used by Multi-Layer Perceptrons. It is a more sophisticated algorithm than steepest descent but requires more computation.

date data
Data that encode a date. This is often in the raw format DDMMYY, but a better one for neural networks is Y Y.Y Y.

field	An aspect of a data set that encodes some feature of the data. This is usually represented by a column in a spreadsheet.
full response	A Kohonen network output function. This gives the output at each of the neurons in the Kohonen layer.
global solution	The best model that can be built for a particular problem, defined as the solution with the lowest error.
hidden layer	A layer of nodes in a neural network that has no direct connections outside the neural network.
historical data	Data that describe a feature you want to model.
input data	Data fields that are being used to learn or to calculate another field.
input data space	A way of looking at problems, in which each input field is viewed as a spatial dimension and each record is viewed as points within the resulting space.
input layer	A layer of neurons in a neural network that takes the input data, and passes them to the hidden layer.
Kohonen networks	An unsupervised neural network technique.
layers	A group of neurons that process in parallel. Neural networks are created from layers of neurons.
learning algorithm	A rule that indicates how learning should take place. The selection of a learning algorithm influences how well a neural network is able to solve a problem.
model	A representation of a problem, allowing targets to be evaluated for a set of inputs. Models can be statistical or neural.
Multi-Layer Perceptron	A supervised neural network. This is the most common neural network technique and is built from several layers of connected nodes.
neighborhood	A group of neurons in a Kohonen network that are associated with each other.

neuron	A small processing element from which a neural network is built. Each neuron performs a simple calculation. It is by arranging neurons in connected layers that neural networks are able to solve complex problems.
nodes	A neuron in an artificial neural network.
normalization	A technique for limiting the variance of a field.
optimization	The methodology for approaching the global solution for a problem.
output data	Another name for target data.
output layer	The final layer of neurons in a neural network. This layer takes input from the hidden layer and generates the output.
overtraining	If training is allowed to progress for too long, overtraining is said to have taken place. In these cases, a neural network loses the ability to generalize.
prediction problems	A problem that produces a real valued output for an example.
principal component analysis	A technique for reducing the dimensionality of a problem.
processing element	A node in an artificial neural network.
Radial Basis Function network	A supervised neural network.
regression	A statistical technique that links input variables using a straight line equation. Regression produces a real valued output for an example.
segmentation	Splitting a data set into a number of groups that share similar features.
Simple Perceptron	The forerunner to the Multi-Layer Perceptron.
steepest descent	A learning algorithm that is used by Multi-Layer Perceptrons. It is a simpler algorithm than conjugate gradient but takes more steps to reach a solution.

suboptimal solution	A stable solution that does not have as low an error as the global solution.
supervised learning	A training process in which a teaching mechanism is used to make a neural network associate targets with inputs. Training data must contain targets for supervised learning to take place.
symbolic data	Data that contain a finite number of symbols, or classes. These data must be properly encoded for a neural network, usually by using 1-of-N encoding.
target data	The field that a neural network is trying to learn.
test data	A set of complete historical data that is kept aside to confirm the performance of an application.
time series forecasting	Using the time dependencies present in a data set to predict future values.
training data	Data records that are used to train a neural network.
transfer function	Another name for the activation function. An element of a neuron in a Multi-Layer Perceptron. A smooth nonlinear function that is used to modify the summed inputs to the neuron.
unsupervised learning	A learning technique in which there is no direct teacher mechanism. The most common unsupervised neural network is the Kohonen network.
validation data	Data that are used to prevent a neural network from overtraining. It is important that the validation data and training data both cover the full range of the problem.
variables	Fields in the data set.
Vector Quantization	A Kohonen network output function. This gives a code number associated with the winning neuron in the Kohonen layer.
weights	The values associated with the connections between nodes in a neural network. Adjusting the weights causes the neural network to learn.
zero mean one standard deviation	A normalization technique that maps the one standard deviation points of a data field to plus and minus one.

Index